Praise for Robin Norwood

"A life-changing book."
—*Erica Jong*

"Really brilliant . . . I absolutely related to it."
—*Marian Keyes,* Mail on Sunday

"Highly recommended."
—Daily Record *(UK)*

Why
Me?
Why
This?
Why
Now?

Why Me? Why This? Why Now?

A Guide to Answering Life's Toughest Questions

Robin Norwood

Jeremy P. Tarcher/Penguin
a member of Penguin Group (USA)
New York

JEREMY P. TARCHER/PENGUIN
Published by the Penguin Group
Penguin Group (USA) LLC
375 Hudson Street
New York, New York 10014

USA · Canada · UK · Ireland · Australia
New Zealand · India · South Africa · China

penguin.com
A Penguin Random House Company

First published in Great Britain in 1994 by Century
First published by Arrow Books in 1995
Reissued by Arrow Books in 2009
First Tarcher/Penguin paperback edition 2013
New introduction by the author © 2013
Copyright © 1994 by Robin Norwood

Most Tarcher/Penguin books are available at special quantity discounts for bulk purchase
for sales promotions, premiums, fundraising, and educational needs. Special books or
book excerpts also can be created to fit specific needs. For details, write:
Special.Markets@us.penguingroup.com.

Library of Congress Cataloging-in-Publication Data

Norwood, Robin.
Why Me? why this? why now? : a guide to answering life's
toughest questions / by Robin Norwood.
p.   cm.
ISBN 978-0-399-16583-2
1. Suffering—Religious aspects—New age movement. 2. Spiritual life—New Age
Movement. 3. New age movement. I. Title.
BP605.N48N67   2013   2013015441
131—dc23

Printed in the United States of America
1 3 5 7 9 10 8 6 4 2

Book design by Chris Welch

This book is dedicated with gratitude to all my teachers.

Contents

Introduction
to the 2013 Edition

A careful rereading of *Why Me? Why This? Why Now?* for the purpose of writing a new introduction made it clear to me that times have indeed changed since the book's first publication twenty years ago. A pertinent example is its earnest treatment of the many necessary lessons then being imparted by the AIDS epidemic. In these intervening years what were at that time almost inconceivable adjustments in consciousness have occured regarding homosexuality, family secrets, and the dying process. All of us are richer, wiser, more compassionate, and considerate precisely because a devastating force touched so many lives that it could not be denied or ignored.

So, times have changed. And yet they haven't . . . not really. Whatever may be the pressing issue at the forefront of the news, the process of unwelcome pressure producing needed change in the individual and throughout humanity goes on as always. If some of the examples in *Why . . . ?* are showing their age a bit, well—that simply proves the case, doesn't it? We've absorbed some necessary lessons and are on to our next ones. There will always be lessons, and there will often be pain we struggle to learn them. I humbly submit that *Why* . . . ? continues to offer a valuable perspective to anyone in any kind of pain.

A different perspective produces different experience even when outer conditions remain the same. Ironically, when our perspective changes for the better, often so eventually do the conditions of our lives.

One of the gifts of age is a wider, or at least a definitely longer, perspective. As I near my seventh decade, I look back on a life that divides itself roughly into three eras lived by three quite dissimilar people. I clearly see that my self-will fueled my first thirty-five years. I single-mindedly pursued whatever goals I thought would bring me happiness. When the results fell short of my expectations, I applied *more* self-will. Eventually a lot of wreckage piled up as life and I collided.

In the fifteen years that followed, I learned that most of my difficulties and nearly all of my unhappiness came from insisting that life go my way. I began to live on life's terms rather than insisting that mine were better. The reward was a serenity I had never before experienced. And that, in turn, has evolved in these most recent years into a nearly constant state of gratitude for all that I've experienced, all that I've learned, and all that I've been able to give back.

Indeed, the deepest gratitude is for what was, at the time, the most unbearable pain because that is where the gifts of this life of mine were hidden. There, in the rubble of mistakes and regrets, were the experience, strength, and hope I later could offer to another whose struggles were as overwhelming as mine had once been.

But make no mistake. Those gifts residing in the pain do not automatically emerge. Without a change of perspective, the rubble remains rubble and we risk becoming buried by an increasingly embittered life.

Anonymous others who had achieved that changed perspective helped me with the same encouragement, reassurance, and guidance that they had, in their turn, been given. It took time but because I was willing, those unwelcome experiences became my greatest treasures. I wrote this book to pass on that gift of a changed perspective as well as my deepened understanding of the purpose and meaning of life, and my rock-solid gratitude for it all.

Although my first book, *Women Who Love Too Much*, has had the lion's share of success in the world, it is this book, *Why . . . ?* that I believe I was born to write. I am so grateful to Tarcher for making it available again so that the gift can be passed on to you.

Introduction
to the 1994 Edition

Why me? Why this? Why now? Who among us hasn't been driven in times of trouble to demand answers to these questions? We search our hearts. We query Life. We rail at God. We rant at any sympathetic listener. *Why?* And the replies that come back—vague, general palliatives that cannot begin to address our particular pain and frustration—feel empty, impersonal, even maddening.

"Time heals all things."

"You're upset now, but you'll get over it."

"It's God's will and not for us to question."

"It's Fate."

"These things just happen."

Perhaps the most impossible bit of advice when we're overwhelmed by our difficulty is "Try not to dwell on it. Thinking about it will only make you feel worse." Words offered by well-meaning friends, helpless in the face of our distress, leave us shipwrecked and unsoothed on the shoals of whatever has gone so very, very wrong. We drag ourselves wearily over the bruising details of our lives until eventually we find that time does indeed heal much after all, though sorrow and suffering have left deep and indelible tracks across the heart.

Still, those questions we once asked silently or cried aloud remain unanswered. When happier times come our need for answers fades—until we face adversity again.

Why me? Why this? Why now? These are questions I often heard as a therapist, and I wondered at the particular nature and timing of my clients' troubles. Many times I've asked these same questions of myself in a life that has had its share of difficulties. But when my own problems weighed heavily, my emotions prevented me from objectively investigating what were in fact very deep questions having enormous implications. And when life was good I was too content to bother.

Life seemed good, indeed, following the publication of my first book, *Women Who Love Too Much*. I was married to an intelligent, successful man who was supportive of my work. I had a flourishing practice as a psychotherapist, was a best-selling author and an internationally recognized authority on relationship addiction. I had been able to take all the pain from years of failure with men and love and, with the help of a spiritual program, distill it into wisdom that saved my life. Now I was helping women everywhere do the same for themselves. It was a time of gratitude for my own recovery and pride in what I was accomplishing out in the world. But this state was not to last much longer.

One day in the fall of 1986, I was returning to California by plane from a speaking engagement when I fell into a casual conversation with the woman seated next to me. As we were chatting, she suddenly peered at me closely.

"How old are you?" she asked in a changed voice.

"I'll be forty-two next July," I answered.

She nodded slowly, continuing to look at me intently. "Your whole life is going to change in the next year," she solemnly informed me.

I was amused. "No, no. You don't understand. It's *already* changed," I told her. "Things have always been so difficult for me, but now they're just *perfect*." I smilingly informed her just how far I'd come in a few short years. "I have a really nice husband now, and I'm truly successful for the first time in my life. Everything's absolutely *perfect*," I repeated proudly.

"It's all going to change," she replied. "Everything's going to go." Then she said, by way of explanation, "I have a gift, you know. I see things."

At that point a flight attendant arrived with our dinners and the conversation never returned to the subject of what my future might hold. But she proved to be absolutely right.

By the following April, I was divorcing my husband, no longer working as a therapist, and although I didn't know it yet, I was seriously ill and slowly dying.

The divorce was my idea, and the only reason I could give at the time was that the marriage was no longer honest for me. I found myself constantly pretending to be the happy person I thought I should be. Every day I remained in this charade meant living a lie and I had to stop. But by doing so, wasn't I letting down all the women who had read my book and believed I was a recovered relationship addict living happily ever after with a nice man? I felt I'd failed my readers.

Ending my career was my idea, as well. For years I had deeply loved my work, but now the passion was utterly gone and I knew that another area of my life was no longer honest. My view of reality was radically changing, and there were deeper truths I wanted to pursue, truths that were taking me far beyond the practice of therapy.

Dying—well, I suppose at some level that was my idea, too. For months my body had battled a raging infection that caused little pain but made me extremely weak. I told myself that my infirmity was probably due to a lingering flu and didn't merit my seeking medical help. Even though at times I could barely walk across a room, I clearly didn't want to know how sick I was. Maybe subconsciously I thought that all my disappointed readers might forgive me if I died.

By the time I finished my second book, which contained my final words on relationship addiction, I felt I had done all I could for my readers. In considerable pain now, I entered the hospital. By this time my closest woman friend had faded out of my life and my children were living in distant cities. Seeing little likelihood of comfort anywhere, I kept my condition to myself. I wasn't at all afraid of dying—just very, very tired, too tired to keep going. I was alone and I wanted out.

The following morning as I was wheeled into surgery, I concentrated on those few persons in my life I still hadn't been able to completely forgive and bless. I tried hard to do so right then, but that wasn't completely honest either, and I was too weak and too weary for lies even to myself. So with deep disappointment in myself and my life, I slipped under the anesthetic.

My disappointment was even greater when I awakened after surgery. My first thought was "Oh, no! I'm still here. Now what am I going to do for the *next* forty-two years?" When the anesthesiologist later informed me cheerfully that the operating room nurses, all of whom had read my book, had been praying that I'd pull through, I thought ungratefully, "Why didn't they mind their own business?" An entire lifetime had come to an end. Why then, hadn't I been allowed to leave?

Perhaps hardest of all was the feeling that I was asking my questions into a void. Throughout the previous seven years I had practiced a program of recovery from relationship addiction based on the same principles used by members of Alcoholics Anonymous and had experienced again and again the welcome comfort and guidance of a Higher Power. Now it seemed that a door had closed, and I was left on the other side with nothing to guide me but that same inconvenient demand for personal honesty that had already cost me most of my identity. Feeling alternately toyed with, abandoned, and betrayed, I didn't yet understand that God is always unknowable and that as we move closer to Him, God moves farther away, drawing us higher and higher as we seek and search and try to follow.

My convalescence was followed by what would ultimately be a seven-year-long period of isolation and reflection. At first I thrashed about trying to find something to do that would give my life focus and purpose. But all my plans, big or small, were thwarted. The days stretched long and empty, and I was plagued with guilt over my inactivity.

Reading books on esoteric subjects that I had never previously given any thought to—astrology, palmistry, tarot, and healing— was my only real interest. Having always believed in reincarnation, I now sought a deeper understanding of corresponding spiritual concepts. My house began to fill with books on related subjects:

the human aura, the various levels of the human energy field, the subtle bodies that interpenetrate the physical body, the chakras or spinning vortices of energy that feed these subtle bodies, thought forms, psychic healing, the dying process, etc.

I discovered in myself a hunger for the profoundly esoteric works of Alice Bailey, a Theosophist who served from the early 1920s to the 1950s as the amanuensis, or channel, for a Tibetan Master. My first taste of these writings was the especially inscrutable *Treatise on Cosmic Fire*, which I came across in the religion section of the public library. Though I found the book nearly incomprehensible, I felt the deepest trust in this Master of the Wisdom, known simply as the Tibetan, and began to study the more than twenty volumes he had dictated to Bailey. I found my empty days filling as I submerged myself in these studies that fed me as nothing else could.

During this period, I felt a need to protect myself from outer influences. Solitude became nearly as necessary to me as air. Having already lived without a television for ten years, I now avoided the radio, magazines, and newspapers as well, insulating myself as completely as I could from the distortions and misconceptions that constitute our shared cultural view of reality. I assiduously avoided everything that might distract me—men, parties, social gatherings, alcohol, caffeine, sugar.

Both my children, now adults, were sympathetic to and interested in the subjects that now consumed me. And gradually, one by one, a few women appeared who were engrossed in quests compatible with mine. Like refugees from a far land, we discovered that we shared a language and perspective, and a tiny handful of rich friendships blossomed.

Occasionally when I've described this period of isolation and reflection to people they have responded with envy, imagining that it must have been a blissfully peaceful idyll. In reality, it was often more like daily torture. I was sitting still, avoiding all of the usual distractions employed by people in this culture *because I had no choice*. None of those distractions *worked* for me any-more. The "hangover" they left me with made employing them too costly. Still, especially in the early years, I was restless, trou-bled, consumed with a need to know where (if anywhere) I was heading and what (if anything) was my purpose. I wasn't yet able to see that now I finally had the time, the detachment, the objec-tivity, and the motivation to explore the nature, timing, and pur-pose of adversity. Now I was free to investigate what I have come to refer to as the "WHY?" behind the "why?"

Today I realize that my studies in the esoteric realm are a di-rect outgrowth of my work in the field of addiction. For many years I had deeply explored relationship addiction and recovery, tracing its origins to unhealthy patterns of relating usually learned while growing up within a dysfunctional family. These patterns were carried over into adult life and unconsciously repeated with partners with whom the old dramas experienced in childhood could be played out again.

But now I wanted to know *why* some of us are born into dys-functional families in the first place? Why is one baby born into an optimal, healthy environment while another enters life facing conditions guaranteed to traumatize? Why are the conditions of life—the quality of our parents, our health, intelligence, eco-nomic strata—meted out so unequally? Are we random victims in a Universal Wild Ride? Or do we have destinies that fit in some ordered way into an Overall Plan? And if we have such a destiny, how can we intuit its direction and make use of that knowledge?

Finally, I was exploring in earnest what I had always believed to be the true and correct focus of psychology: the study (-ology) of the soul (psyche). I began to understand how each of us is born with a specific "energy package," traced in the palm and depicted in the horoscope—a basic energetic structure that causes us to have certain kinds of encounters and experiences at certain times as our life unfolds.

Enthralled, I sought out and studied with several psychics and healers who helped me perceive and work with the subtle energies that make up this package. I practiced with other students, reading and interacting with their energy fields (or auras) in order to facilitate various kinds of healing. I met others who, like myself, had never considered themselves psychic. Yet together we were accomplishing some extraordinary things and sharing some extraordinary discoveries that contributed greatly to my understanding.

Gradually, as my worldview underwent this profound paradigmatic shift, all of the many and varied experiences of my life took on both a pattern and a meaning. I no longer saw myself and others on an unfolding ribbon stretching from birth to death, marked along the way with various events, happy or unhappy, welcomed or dreaded. Rather, I was beginning to intuit a vast background of unfolding evolutionary themes operating in each individual life. My understanding was at once objective and subjective. Having worked so often with those who felt lost and alone, and having spent so much of my life feeling that way, too, my studies were suddenly delivering into my hands a map that, in addition to describing the surrounding territory, also displayed the vital orienting red arrow indicating "You are here." I saw my place and my purpose in the Universe, recognized my flaws and failures and frustrations as the necessities they were, the *gifts* they were. This deeper understanding of the overall schema and my contribution to it gave me what all my involvement with psychology and its emphasis on "fixing the problem" hadn't. It gave me back to myself. And it allowed me to understand the purpose of suffering.

In this book I offer to you what these years of intense study and reflection and attention to subtle energies have taught me regarding the gifts of adversity. That you are drawn to this book at this time may signify that you, too, are undergoing the same paradigmatic shift I did. Like Columbus as he noted increasing evidence that the world was not flat but round, you may be gathering experiences and perceptions that are bringing about an equally drastic revision of your own worldview. Your emerging comprehension of new dimensions may require a different kind of map, one that accommodates and reflects this changed perspective.

It is deliberate that many stories herein of men and women struggling with various kinds of problems also include these people's paranormal experiences and perceptions. As the cultural climate is expanding its acceptance of such experiences, more and more people are coming forward to talk about them. I found that once I opened myself to the subtler dimensions of reality, many people spontaneously confided their personal experiences with the paranormal to me. If these kinds of events have occurred in your own life, you will find the inclusion of such stories validating. If they are not yet part of your experience, I hope you will read with tolerance. By doing so, you very well may awaken to these subtler dimensions yourself, for as we enter the New Age each of us is expanding our powers of perception. Along with acknowledgment of these dimensions and occurrences comes the possibility of understanding much that otherwise appears inexplicable and unjust.

You may find some of the concepts explored herein unfamiliar. If so, have patience with yourself and your understanding. You may find it helpful to reread the book again after some time has passed. Doing so will show you how much your comprehension has deepened. This book, by changing your attitudes and perceptions, can truly change your life. Let it guide you to discover and appreciate your unique place and purpose; find within it your own personal map complete with red arrow giving you your bearings through the affirming and reassuring message "You are here."

But how, you may be wondering, does gaining this expanded perspective *help* you, struggling as you must be with whatever personal issues have prompted you to pick up this particular book at this particular time? When you are seeking help and comfort, why should it be necessary to alter your worldview, to regard your difficulties against such an immense and seemingly irrelevant backdrop? The answer is simple. By doing so, your pain and your psychic wounds can be understood and thereby healed.

True healing from any crisis occurs in stages. While we are still in the throes of our distress we are comforted by stories of others who have similarly suffered, stories that reassure us we are not alone either in our condition or in our reaction to it. You may very well find not only your circumstances but your response to them reflected here to some degree.

Next, as our acute emotional crisis passes, we have a need to begin to make sense of what we have been through in terms of the overall design or fabric of our life. We wonder, if we believe in a Weaver, did His hand simply falter on the shuttle, dropping some threads so irrevocably that the tapestry of our life is now forever flawed? Or has a new depth and richness been added now that the design has taken an unexpected turn? For it is never the event but rather how it is handled and *defined* that determines its ultimate effect on us, positive or negative. This book can be of help to you in reframing your greatest difficulties so that their gifts, possibly still hidden from your view, may be discerned.

Finally, when we can use whatever difficulties we have experienced in order to help others, then all our suffering and struggles are raised up and given purpose and dignity even beyond ourselves. They are redeemed. This book may be able to help you understand the esoteric principle of sacrifice as you have perhaps heretofore unconsciously expressed it in some important dimension of your life. The principle of sacrifice is operating whenever others learn a better way through our suffering. But it is not our suffering that is the gift. It is our healing. Spiritual development and healing are essentially the same thing. Through our suffering *and* healing, we help to enlighten humanity as a whole. Our own personal tragedy, regarded from this perspective, precipitates a deepened comprehension of the true meaning and purpose of individual existence, intertwining our personal healing with the healing of the entire planet.

What does this healing require of us? Most of all, a willingness to open to a view of reality that includes subjective and as yet scientifically "unprovable" truths of the heart and the soul. Healing comes about through a change of consciousness, a change of heart; through forgiveness of others, forgiveness of ourselves, forgiveness of Life and of God. Healing comes when we relinquish our beliefs about what the conditions of our lives *should* have been and become willing to accept and eventually even appreciate what simply *is*.

By opening to a view of adversity as a path to our healing, we can feel trust even in times of despair. We can trust not only that the pain will pass, but that our suffering has meaning and purpose and dignity. It is because I trust in your healing and my healing and the healing of the body of humanity of which we each comprise a part that I offer here for your consideration some possible answers to those impossible questions: Why me? Why this? Why now?

One

Why Is This Happening to Me?

Joanna lay tensely quiet on the chiropractor's table, staring up at the mobile dangling above her as it dipped and spun lazily in the soft breeze from the open window overhead. I had already learned a bit about this young woman who had hobbled into the office on crutches, worried that a sprained ankle was "staying too swollen too long." Now I sat at her feet, the middle fingers of each of my hands gently resting on opposite sides of her bruised, blue ankle.

Doing this was part of my job assisting a chiropractor who in exchange was treating me for a knee injury that had failed to respond to traditional medical treatment. The doctor, known locally for her unusual healing gifts, had a mixed clientele and used various approaches to augment her chiropractic skills: energy work, crystals, and visualizations. Working with her was an opportunity for me to learn more about nontraditional healing, and it was under her direction that I was now doing "energy work" on Joanna.

My fingers slowly moved along a series of paired dots made with a felt-tipped pen by the doctor on either side of Joanna's ankle and foot. My task was to feel for the two pulses, one under the middle finger of each of my hands, and to hold them until they synchronized both in rhythm and strength. It was a technique we used to help muscle spasms release, but it was also helpful in relieving areas of congestion and inflammation due to injuries. Sometimes a patient's pulses would line up quickly. At other times they would be sluggish. How readily synchronization could be affected was often related to the patient's psychological state, and since Joanna's pulses were slow in coming around, I broached the subject of her injury.

"So how did this happen?" I asked. She rolled her head and let out an exasperated sigh.

"Oh, it was so *stupid!* All I did was walk across the kitchen floor. I was wearing tennis shoes and my foot just stuck to the floor while the rest of me kept going. And now I'm on crutches for eight more weeks." Her voice caught as she added, "I can't do *anything.*"

"It's hard when life slows us down like that," I said, reminded of how much my knee injury had taught me about holding still. Beneath my fingers Joanna's pulses were still refusing to coordinate.

"What would you be doing right now if this hadn't happened?" I asked.

"Oh, ordinarily nothing that important. It's just that the timing is so terrible." Again the catch in her voice.

"It's worse than some other time?"

A pause. A hand raised to brush away some tears. "Yes, it is. It's about the worst time possible."

I waited, passed her a tissue as she was openly crying now, and then resumed my work. After a moment she continued.

"My mother has cancer. She's *dying*. And she's at home because she wants it that way. We, she and I, thought it could work with help from the visiting nurses, but now . . ."

I moved my hands to another pair of marks and asked, "Is there anyone else who can help?"

"Well, there's my father, of course, but they've never gotten along."

"They fight?" I asked, bluntly. Joanna hesitated only for a moment.

"No, not really. More like that real old-fashioned kind of marriage where the husband goes out and works and the wife does everything to make him comfortable at home and he never notices. I think my mother finally got so tired of not being appreciated that something in her closed off toward him. They both seem to live inside separate boxes, never touching, not physically, not emotionally."

I moved my hands again. "What's he doing now that she's so ill?"

A long pause. Then, almost reluctantly, "He's helping. I mean he's actually taking care of her, asking her all the time what she needs and what she'd like and trying to make her comfortable."

"And your mother's reaction?"

"For the longest time she wouldn't ask him for anything. They're one of those couples who, you know, don't speak to each other. They talk to everyone else but never to each other. They do that 'Tell your mother . . .' or 'Tell your father . . .' when the other one is *right there*. It's awful."

Joanna was more composed as she related the story of her parents' decades-long cold war.

"When my mother learned she had cancer, that's when she

spoke to him again. I was there at the hospital. She looked straight at him and said, 'Ray, I'm dying.' He started to cry and said, 'Let me help you,' and she said, 'No. Joanna will take care of me.' And I did. I took care of her"—she gestured down at her ankle and was crying again—"but now I can't."

"No," I said. "But your father can. Maybe that's what all this is about. Look, Joanna," I said, touching the mobile that turned above her. "Imagine that this mobile represents your family. Each family member maintains a certain set position or role creating a delicate balance. Your mother's illness is like a strong breeze that came along and shook everything up." I blew hard at the mobile and it jiggled in response. "But still the essential balance would have remained the same except . . ." I then reached up and un- hooked one of the mobile's dangling figures. As I did so, the en- tire structure tilted to compensate. "This is what happened in your family. Your injury removed you from your usual position in between your parents and pushed these two stubborn people into having to deal with each other: I think maybe it's a blessing."

The mobile resettled itself at a rakish angle before Joanna finally sighed deeply and said, "All those years I guess I thought it was my dad's fault. I was always kind of on her side. But I watched the way she punished him when he tried to help in the hospital and then at home. She wouldn't let anything he did be right. But he just kept trying. I was amazed. And finally she melted a little bit. Now I go visit and Dad waits on us both and teases us and even makes Mom laugh. And when he gets me alone he says, 'You know I love your mother. I've always loved her.' And I say, 'Tell her!' And he says, 'I'm trying, I'm trying.'"

The pulses under my fingertips had begun to synchronize as we talked. By the time I finished my work, the swelling had visibly diminished. Both energy and circulation were moving more efficiently, but Joanna hardly seemed to notice.

"So I don't have to feel terrible that I haven't been there for her? You know, I think I even knew it was better that Dad was doing everything and I was on the sidelines. But I felt so guilty."

"You had your familiar part to play and not to do so was hard on you. Even the word *familiar* comes from *family*, from what we're used to. I imagine only something as disabling as this injury could have kept you out of the picture." We were both smiling when I handed Joanna her crutches.

Had Joanna not understood her long-standing role of running interference between her parents, she may well have been consumed by guilt over her inability to keep the promise she had made her mother. Joanna's healing came about when she gained a more balanced view of her parents' relationship and realized that her role in the family as her mother's supporter and comforter actually enabled the couple to continue to feud. Their reconciliation relieved her of an inappropriate measure of responsibility for her mother's happiness, a responsibility she might otherwise have carried long after her mother's death.

Her father, too, underwent a healing. My guess is that prior to the crisis of her illness, Joanna's mother had punished her husband daily for some long-ago indiscretion. Their interactions had so crystallized that both were imprisoned in their stereotypical behaviors of many years' duration. When the double crisis of her mother's cancer and Joanna's injury coincided, the fact that this man persevered in his efforts to break free from his role of indifference and offer his wife love over and over until she could accept it constituted both his own healing and, finally, the possibility of a positive resolution to their relationship.

> When Joanna returned to the office two months later for a final checkup, she took me aside for a moment to tell me her mother had passed away at home a few weeks before.
>
> "It was really beautiful. We were all there. My husband. My boys. But at the very end she wanted to be alone with Dad. Can you imagine? The same man she didn't talk to for all those years! We were waiting in the living room when Dad finally came out. He said, 'She's gone now. But it's okay. She knew I loved her.'" Crying now and unable to say more, Joanna squeezed my hand and turned to walk quickly out of the office.

Healing that goes beyond the physical

What is healing? Is a person who is physically ill healed only when that illness is alleviated or cured? Or is it possible that not only Joanna and her father underwent a healing, but so did her mother? Did the woman, through forgiving her husband and opening her heart to love, heal even though she lost her physical body through death?

In this book we will come to understand how our entire being, both physical and nonphysical, is affected by every positive change in consciousness. This is the esoteric view of evolution as it applies to the human race. If the case of Joanna's mother is seen from this perspective, a greatly expanded understanding of her death becomes possible, a view Joanna seemed intuitively to grasp. Her mother's healing into greater love was of deeper significance than her physical death, painful as that loss was. The dying woman's transformation permitted an expansion of consciousness in her husband and daughter as well.

Many of life's difficulties, when viewed from an esoteric perspective, reveal the opportunities they offer for the kind of deep healing that occurred in the example above. It might be helpful at this point to offer a somewhat radical redefinition of healing, one that recognizes that there exist subtler, more profound, and more important levels on which to be healed than the physical. This redefinition consists of six basic premises:

1. Deep healing always involves a change of heart and therefore an expansion of consciousness.
2. The cure of a physical condition or illness does not necessarily imply that meaningful healing has taken place.
3. The continuation of a physical condition or illness, even if death eventuates, does not necessarily imply that meaningful healing has *not* taken place.
4. In the emotional realm, the greater the trauma, the greater the potential for meaningful healing.
5. At the level of thought, the greater the distortion in the belief system, the greater the healing, should that distortion be corrected.
6. The healing of the individual affects the healing of the entire body of humanity; the healing of the body of humanity affects the healing of the entire planet.

We can accept this six-point redefinition of healing when what we call personal tragedies are viewed as taking place in a wider context, one that includes past, present, and future and all family members and friends, society as a whole, and ultimately the entire human race. This perspective also requires our acknowledgment that the nonphysical parts of us, our emotional and mental aspects, may be in even greater need of healing than the physical.

An esoteric view of human existence

The following discussion of the subtle bodies, death, and the soul is a necessarily brief overview that cannot begin to do justice to these vast and complex subjects. Still, such an introduction is important to a more complete understanding of adversity and healing, the subjects of this book. As you read the following few pages, don't worry if the concepts discussed seem alien and elusive. This background will still help you understand our place in the Universe and our relationship to the soul.

We must begin by recognizing that we are more than a physical body. The human aura or "energy package" in which we dwell while alive on Earth includes several dimensions of reality beyond those we perceive with our five senses.

Underlying and interpenetrating the physical body are increasingly subtler bodies comprised of increasingly subtler grades of matter. These bodies are: our etheric body, interpenetrating the physical body as its energetic blueprint and made up of vibrating lines of light; our astral (or emotional) body, comprised of matter from the astral level of the Universal energy field—and full of flowing colors and flashes of light as its highly volatile substance responds to and reflects our changing emotions; and our mental body, made up of two levels of matter: lower mental matter, vivified by gaining knowledge but tinged with emotion, and higher mental matter, which is the realm of pure thought, wisdom, and understanding, the level on which the soul dwells. The soul is seated within the human aura in the area of the manubrium or the thymus gland but exists in the extremely fine matter of the higher mental level of the human energy field. It serves as a bridge of consciousness between our physical-plane existence and the Spirit or Force behind Creation.

As we evolve, we first must gain control of the physical body. Then we must harness our emotions through discipline. And finally the emotionally conditioned matter of the lower mental body is gradually shed and we become more focused at the higher mental level. As our higher mental body develops through this focusing, so does our capacity to experience conscious contact with the soul and with the Plan for our lives.

As what we call death occurs, the energetic thread connecting the soul to the physical body is broken. When the soul abandons its connection with this physical body that has served as its outpost on the physical plane, it withdraws the unifying force that heretofore prevented the dissolution of the physical body and the separation of the subtle bodies from the physical. The etheric portion of the physical body begins to separate from the denser vehicle, the finer etheric matter gradually lifting off. Onlookers frequently note a definite translucence on the face of the recently deceased, light around the body, and a feeling of peace in the room, all due to this finer energy permeating the area as it is freed from the dense physical body. This etheric component usually dissolves within one to three days after the energetic thread, also known as the silver cord, is broken.

Just as, in the natural course of things, the physical matter that comprised the physical body would be gradually reabsorbed by the physical plane, so the astral, and lower and higher mental materials that comprised the individual's subtle bodies while alive are reabsorbed into their appropriate energetic levels of the Universal energy field after death. All that has been garnered through experience during the just-completed lifetime is absorbed into the appropriate subtle plane. Matter of an emotional nature is absorbed into the astral plane, while the knowledge and wisdom gained are received by the lower and higher mental planes. Because whatever we have gained is thus harvested by the soul at the completion of each of our lifetimes; the development, refinement, and purification of these subtle bodies is a major purpose of ephemeral human existence on the Earth plane. *It is our contribution to the evolution of the Universe.*

We are told by clairvoyants, whose vision allows them to perceive finer states of matter, that as we achieve greater understanding, forgiveness, and freedom from selfish illusions and desires our energy bodies are clarified, intensified, and expanded. Most such expansions are brought about through our struggles with the limitations we encounter dwelling in the dense physical body on the Earth plane.

Some of these struggles and their effects on our subtle bodies and thus on our higher Selves will be described throughout this book. We will see some specific ways in which the difficult conditions we face enable us to achieve a more complete rapport with our emanating source, the soul—and how this in turn makes possible the eventual return of the soul, enriched by the same process of *expression, experience*, and *expansion*, to its own source, Spirit.

Adversity as a catalyst for change

Darren is a young man who, until being diagnosed as HIV-positive at twenty-one, had been a production assistant in the television industry, living and working very much in the fast lane. That personal suffering can precipitate a healing of the subtler dimensions of one's being and produce greater rapport with one's higher Self or soul is well illustrated by Darren's story, which follows:

> I was diagnosed two years ago after I had lost a lot of weight and had thrush. Even though the symptoms were pretty obvious, I was shocked. I ran with this crowd where no one had gotten sick. We all thought it wasn't going to happen to us. I was the first.
>
> They put me on AZT and since then I've been in pretty good shape most of the time. I get tired easily and I've been back in the hospital twice, but I can pretty much take care of myself right now. But my whole lifestyle has changed. It always used to be "Where's the party?" It was always happening out there somewhere, and you had to run real fast to try to find it, to be sure not to miss it. A lot of drugs, all this real trendy stuff, a *lot* of alcohol. But when I was first in the hospital this guy I didn't even know, Roger, came to see me. He'd had his diagnosis for four years. He told me he'd help

me all he could and when he couldn't there'd be other people who could.

And then this really big change began happening for me. When the AZT started working and I felt better, I didn't go back to running around. Roger would take me to meet other people like me, like us, you know, who'd been diagnosed, and we'd just be with each other. We'd *talk* to one another and look at each other and say, "How are you doing today?" and *listen* for the answer, and all of a sudden whatever I'd always been looking for wasn't out there anymore. It was right here with these people, and I could tell it was the same for them. Some of them are so sick or maybe their families won't have anything to do with them or they haven't got any money or they're just plain scared. But there's this attitude, where we give each other what we can and nobody has to deal with it alone.

We've opened a house here in town for people with AIDS who have nowhere to go and *everything* has been donated. People still come to the door and just say, "Here."

It sounds really funny to say I'm grateful for this disease but in a way I am. It's taught me how to live. And not just me; my family, too. My grandmother's the one in our family with all the money, a real matriarch. She's always been critical of my friends and lifestyle. In fact, she used to accuse me of *trying* to get AIDS. Well, when she learned about my diagnosis, she ranted and raved and all she could think about was what other people would say. But when I went back into the hospital this last time, she came to see me and told me I could come live in her guest house and she'd cook for me. And she does. For my friends, too, who need to stay if they're sick and the AIDS shelter is full. And she's donated so much to the shelter and to other AIDS patients. She's changed so much. Sometimes I think that's what this disease is all about. It's working on everybody, making them love more and share more and be more tolerant.

You will note that Darren was accused by his grandmother of behaving as though he wanted to get AIDS, and that when he did contract the disease, this careless and hedonistic young man immediately settled quite naturally into a life of service. I sensed in talking with him that he abandoned his former lifestyle not with regret but rather with relief, with a sense that now he was at last able to reunite with his higher Self and higher purpose. This response, though by no means universal among AIDS patients, is nevertheless so common as to suggest that for many of those stricken, the disease is the key and the catalyst that enables them to express a profound commitment to help reach and teach, through their suffering, those whose lives they touch. Perhaps, for many with AIDS, this high purpose is their very reason for being here in this body in this lifetime.

What AIDS is teaching us

By now the agony of the AIDS epidemic has touched every one of us to some degree. And yet, in all its tragic dimensions, it is also, as Darren so wisely noted, healing us as well. No epidemic in history has combined the factors that AIDS does: the long duration of the disease, the fact that most of its victims are young and socially active, its association in the mind of the public with the male homosexual population, and the fact that it is commonly transmitted sexually. These factors are working together to bring about a revolution in personal and social attitudes, behaviors, and values. Ultimately, humanity as a whole is changing in several ways.

As with the creation of a diamond from coal, transformation in the human being usually requires sufficient time and sufficient pressure. This disease provides many of those who contract it with enough of both to bring about the kind of reorientation in personal values experienced by Darren. What had been for him essentially a self-centered, sensation-seeking existence evolved, through the pressure of the disease and the influence of Roger's example, into a life oriented toward greater service to others. And so Darren's life, like Roger's, became an example of a higher principle at work.

Who can say where the ripple effect ends? This is not, after all, a disease that happens in isolation. Most of those stricken are in the prime of life, with parents still living and a wide circle of friends and associates. Every patient's condition, any patient's *transformation* affects many others. The challenge facing Darren's grandmother because of the combined stigma of her grandson's homosexuality and his disease is faced by many who know and care about someone with AIDS. It is often a test of their values and priorities and courage in facing public prejudice. That this imperious dowager chose to love and help her grandson and others like him rather than abandon him out of pride and fear of censure is as wondrous an about-face as Darren's own.

Further, the fact that AIDS is associated by the general public with male homosexuals, a group widely derided and denigrated, is producing a particularly poignant situation. Consider the level of love and caring that the gay community has offered to those of its members who are sick and dying. This caring and compassion has been extended to heterosexual persons with AIDS and their families. Our nation's gay community has made a commitment, in the face of overwhelming pressures, to give whatever help possible so that no one shall die alone. Their support groups and networks of services for patients and their loved ones; the dignity and courage demonstrated in the face of so much illness, so much death; the amazing ability to stay open and loving—all this has become an ongoing example and inspiration to the medical community, to family members and friends, and to society in general.

Whether or not we personally know someone with this disease, AIDS is affecting all of us in the realm of our sexual attitudes and often our sexual activity as well. Those of us who lived through the fifties, sixties, and seventies realize how drastically sexual behavior and mores changed in this country within one brief generation. The ideal of one partner for life was abruptly abandoned in favor of wider sexual experimentation as the availability of birth control that was *nonintrusive to the sex act* coincided with an overall social revolution. Suddenly spontaneous sexual relations between uncommitted partners appeared to be a virtually consequence-free option. So-called free sex became more than an option: it was a way of proving we weren't sexually paralyzed puritans. Strangers joined their bodies whether or not they could comfortably meet each other's eyes in anything other than seductive glances. Often such liaisons required quantities of alcohol and other drugs to quiet qualms and inhibitions.

We've tried our best, but for some of us, men as well as women,

casual sex has never really been casual. Perhaps through AIDS
we are recognizing that it isn't intended to be.

When two people are involved in the act of consensual sex, all
of their bodies merge. Their physical/etheric bodies, their emotional or astral bodies, and their mental bodies all inter-penetrate.
The shape of the heart, traditionally associated with love, actually
depicts the overlapping and merging of the auras or egg-shaped
energy fields of two persons in love. Whether they are bonded by
love or not, such merging of their energy fields occurs during
the sex act. Indeed, it is taught esoterically that one opens one's
soul—the highest part of oneself, the part that is connected to
God—to the partner during intercourse. Hence the risk of psychic damage unless there is an attitude of caring and concern for
each other's well-being. If either person has a negative, hostile, or
indifferent attitude, or a desire to exploit the partner, there is
wounding on the energetic level.

I need to emphasize here that although the frequently exploitive attitudes of men and the resulting damage to women's self-
esteem are widely recognized, it is less commonly admitted that
women may be equally exploitive with men. Some of the negative
impulses that may motivate a woman before and during the
sex act are economic aspirations, a desire to experience power
through her ability to attract a man, or a need to subjugate a man
to her wishes. When any of these attitudes are present, men are
psychically wounded. And of course these themes can occur as
well in relations between same-sex partners. Frequently when
there is no real affection between two people who become sexually involved, both are operating from some degree of negative
motivation and thereby both are damaged.

Today the fear of contracting AIDS has provided a powerful constraint to casual sex and has severely inhibited involvement with more than one partner at a time. The specter of AIDS is causing more and more would-be lovers to ask themselves "How well do I really know this person? How much trust do I feel here?" And the use of a condom, so necessary today for the protection of both partners, creates an especially awkward hiatus in the process of lovemaking between first-time or casual lovers, a tiny moment of truth in the process of being swept away, allowing one's deeper feelings to prevail over physical sensation.

And so the AIDS crisis serves to make us more conscious of what we are doing and why we are doing it, and—ultimately—greater consciousness is ever the goal. Today we have the freedom to find our own way while the disease of AIDS disciplines us to behave responsibly toward ourselves and those with whom we are involved.

The story of Joanna and her parents well illustrates the first three premises in the radical redefinition of healing presented here:

1. Deep healing always involves a change of heart and therefore an expansion of consciousness.
2. The cure of a physical condition or illness does not necessarily imply that meaningful healing has taken place.
3. The continuation of a physical condition or illness, even if death eventuates, does not necessarily imply that meaningful healing has *not* taken place.

Darren's story and the general discussion of AIDS help clar-
ify the fourth and fifth premises:

4. In the emotional realm, the greater the trauma, the greater
   the potential for meaningful healing.
5. At the level of thought, the greater the distortion in the belief system, the greater the healing, should that distortion
   be corrected.

Now consider the sixth premise:

6. The healing of the individual affects the healing of the entire body of humanity; the healing of the body of humanity
   affects the healing of the entire planet.

Reflect on it as you read the following.

AIDS from a planetary perspective

When the entire planet is affected by a condition such as AIDS,
one approach to understanding the process under way is to consider the astrological forces at work, especially those of the outer
planets, whose cycles are slow and affect mass consciousness. As-
trologically, Pluto, the slowest moving of the known planets in
our solar system, entered Scorpio, the sign over which it rules, in
late 1983. At that time the epidemic dimensions of AIDS were
beginning to be recognized worldwide. For most people who
study astrology, it became apparent that AIDS was a very "Pluto
in Scorpio" manifestation, an implacable force for transformation.

Pluto, named for the god of the underworld, is associated with all that is hidden or secret, with the genitals, with genital diseases, with elimination, and with death. It is the planet affiliated with psychotherapy, with endings and new beginnings, with transformation, and with rebirth. Pluto's power, according to astrology, works relentlessly to exhume what is buried in the individual psyche or the culture at large, bringing it into the light. It works to heal the individual soul and transform cultural consciousness. However, the process by which its ends are accomplished can be excruciating.

Scorpio is the sign related to desire of all kinds, but especially to sexual desire and the desire to reform the self and others. Obviously then, the concentrated energy of Pluto in Scorpio creates a force to be reckoned with.

Desire, sex, death, and secrets. Exhumation, elimination, transformation, regeneration. These are powerful forces that disturb our peace, disrupt our lives, dismantle our defenses. It has been stated that our entire planet has AIDS, and this refers not only to the worldwide presence of the epidemic. It is a penetrating expression of the fact that we are all involved and we are all implicated; that each of us is sick and all of us need healing; that we don't know how to live, we don't know how to love, and we don't know how to die. But we're learning—and AIDS is helping teach us through its power.

AIDS is forcing all of us to become more conscious of death and the process of dying. In the midst of life we are asked to face the death of a friend, a relative, a celebrity we admire; to open to another's transition and participate from the heart. When we are helping someone with AIDS, we're being helped as well to discover that we intuitively know how to give comfort and care. I've been told by several people that they learned to follow their intuition while nursing a loved one with AIDS, that toward the end they simply lay next to the person, holding and soothing, sometimes with words, sometimes by singing or humming. When the end was near, some of these caretakers were able to urge softly that the patient let go or go on to the light. These techniques often helped facilitate a very peaceful transition for the dying patient and were deeply comforting as well to those who participated at the time of death. One young woman dying of AIDS had nightly visits from friends who had become devoted to caring for her during her illness. A male friend would hold her feet and very gently rub them while his wife read poetry and sang to her. One night after she had slipped into a coma, her mother came to her bedside and held her and told her that if it was time to go and she was ready, they would all help her, lifting her up out of her body with their thoughts. Then her father came to tell her he loved her. Fifteen minutes later she was gone. I attended a remarkably beautiful memorial service for this young woman, and her passing had clearly shed light on all those whose lives she had touched. Each person, through intimate involvement with her dying, had been moved to reevaluate what kind of event death really is. The result was less fear, greater acceptance and peace, and even a sense of wonder.

The body of humanity, indeed the entire planet, is undergoing an initiation in sex, death, and regeneration, an initiation that requires we revise our attitudes and behaviors regarding each of these crucial issues.

The soul's view of adversity

Darren, himself transformed by a disease that is working to transform us all—should he be pitied or applauded? We may be tempted to focus on the tragic aspects of his condition. But the soul, whose purpose is to bring about our greater understanding, forgiveness, and love, recognizes Darren's triumph as well as his sacrifice.

And Joanna, forced out of the picture while her feuding parents faced her mother's terminal illness together—was that sprained ankle a cruel trick of Fate or a gift from her soul so that her mother, in dying, could open to love?

Everywhere that we see adversity, the soul sees the opportunity for our healing, expansion, and enlightenment. This was brought home to me after a friend of mine, while lying passively on the table during a healing session with me, found herself consciously experiencing a realm other than the physical. Seated before her was a white-robed being whom she immediately knew to be a Guide. He greeted her warmly and invited her questions. Having known poor health herself and having a sister with a terminal illness, she asked if there would be much more suffering in her life. The Guide's gentle answer was, "Of course, my dear. It is necessary. It hammers you."

After the healing session as we discussed what had happened, we both were struck by the power of her Guide's answer: "It hammers you." I thought of an abalone steak, pounded until it is tender and sweet, or metal made stronger each time it is thrust into the fire and then struck on the anvil. Are we each being sweetened and tenderized and yet made stronger, too, as we are hammered? And what do the ways in which we are tried and tested say about us as individuals?

Carl Jung made the trenchant observation that "a person's life is characteristic of that person." Our dilemmas, our difficulties and predicaments and *how we face and handle them* define who we are and why we're here and what we're trying to achieve through earth-plane existence. The personality too often judges individual worth by status and security and outer signs of material achievement, but the soul gives clues to the individual's mettle through the tasks and challenges it assigns. We mistakenly believe that happiness, comfort, ease, security, and status are the goal, but the soul has another agenda altogether. It cares nothing for the personality's suffering, only that there be the refinement, the strengthening, and the purification so that the personality is rendered worthy to serve the soul's purpose. Whenever we ask "Why is this happening to me?" we must try to remember that our happiness, comfort, ease, security, and status don't purify, don't strengthen or refine.

But being hammered in the fire does.

Two

What Is My Body Trying to Tell Me?

G ary was another of the chiropractor's patients, an avid bodybuilder with a friendly, puppy dog grin that belied the aggression implied by all those bulging muscles. He had come to the office because of a mysterious recurring pain in one of his knees that was preventing him from doing the weight training and other sports he enjoyed. Though he had rested his knee for more than a week, he reported impatiently that the pain hadn't lessened.

"I want it fixed," he stated adamantly as he lay on the table. We talked while I worked at releasing some of the muscle spasms in his neck and shoulders before the doctor came to examine him. I had learned always to ask what patients would be doing if there were no pain, because so often the clues to the body's breakdown or revolt lay in what they reported.

Gary's typical day included several classes in hotel and restaurant management at the community college, a two-hour workout at the gym, then a long evening working as a bartender at a popular restaurant on the beach. On weekends after catching up on his homework, he did the maintenance work at his apartment building in partial payment of his rent, then either roller-skated at the beach or worked out at the gym before going to work. Tucked in around the edges of all this activity was an involvement with a steady girlfriend.

I wanted to know more about this incredible round of constant activity, but my first question was, "Do you like your work?" After years of experience in the field of addiction, I always wondered what role alcohol played in a person's life.

"Bartending? Oh, it's okay," he answered. "I want to have a restaurant of my own someday, so it's good experience, but it's a drag watching people drink too much, smoke too much. They trash their bodies but they keep on going. I take good care of mine and look what happens!"

"I don't know, Gary," I responded. "With your schedule, it's kind of like having a car you take out and drive six hundred miles every day."

"Well, I like to keep busy." He was a little defensive. "And I don't drink or smoke like practically everybody else. I work hard to stay healthy." He gestured angrily at his knee. "This shouldn't be happening to me."

"Does the rest of your family feel the same way about taking care of themselves as you do?" I asked.

"I wouldn't exactly say so." Gary's voice was heavy with irony. "My dad drank so much it finally killed him. And my brother's doing his best to follow in his footsteps."

"And your mother?"

"Oh, my mom's great. She's in Colorado right now, studying to be a chiropractor." He grinned. "She's the one who told me to come in here." He seemed to feel the need to explain more.

"You know, my mom put up with a lot of hell for a lot of years. When my dad died there was a little money and she took it and got out. I think it's great. In some ways I wish I could do the same, but I just feel like I've got to keep an eye on my brother. He's my twin. Not identical, but still . . ." There was a quiet moment while Gary's sense of responsibility battled with his yearning for freedom.

After a while I said, "Your mom put up with a lot, but what about you? It's affected you, too, you know."

"I just don't think about it," he answered flatly. "I keep busy and I don't think about it."

"Gary, what if your body's asking you to think about it? What if your knee won't let you keep getting stronger on the outside while you ignore whatever's going on inside?"

There was an uncomfortable pause while I felt Gary's overdeveloped neck muscles tense up another notch under my hands. Then suddenly his resistance melted, his whole body softened. He nearly sighed.

"That's exactly what my girlfriend says. My mom, too. It's funny. I've been seeing these posters at school for a lecture series on adult children of alcoholics. There's this list of characteristics that you develop from growing up with someone who drinks and a lot of them fit for me, like having an overdeveloped sense of responsibility and taking care of everybody else first, or feeling guilty if you stand up for yourself, or not knowing what you feel or how to express it. Anyway, I've been sort of wanting to go to a meeting, but I guess I've been too scared to take the time." He gave a little chuckle. "So you think my knee did this on purpose, huh? Because those lectures are right when I usually work out. . . ."

How the body serves consciousness

Can it be possible that Gary's knee conspired with his higher Self to bring him in touch with those subtler levels within him that needed attention? Again and again while I worked with patients at the chiropractor's office, I watched the principle of *synchronicity* at work. Carl Jung introduced this concept to explain the causes behind coincidence, the reason for events that we would ordinarily attribute to chance but that seem because of their significance to be predestined. Often such events are experienced as serendipitous: a chance occurrence that results in one's being put in touch with obscure sources of much-needed information, for instance, or in finding an old friend after years of separation.

A remarkable episode of this kind took place one day when I attempted to dial a friend. A young woman answered the phone, and when I asked for Margaret she hesitated and then replied, "Do you mean Peggy?" Thinking that perhaps she referred to Margaret by that nickname, I said, "Well, this is Robin Norwood. I'm calling for Margaret." Then the voice exclaimed, "Robin! This is Susan!"

Now I recognized her voice and realized I had reached the person with whom I had been best friends during grammar school. We had long since lost touch. Now she was visiting her sister Peggy.

It was all thoroughly surprising, the more so because the previous night I'd had a vivid dream about Susan in which I saw her going to Hawaii. When I told her this she laughed and said, "I am, next week!" I described how in my dream she flew over to the islands but took a ship back, and she replied that those were her plans exactly! Here were too many coincidences to be explained in any way except by the principle of synchronicity.

If synchronicity is the explanation for occurrences too significant to be coincidental, then it certainly can be used to understand the timing of Gary's painful knee or Joanna's sprained ankle. Both injuries created an almost magical opportunity for inner change and healing to take place.

Esoterically it is taught that every illness, every injury, every experience of suffering serves ultimately to cleanse and to purify. Though we may not always understand exactly how this takes place, if we keep this teaching in mind then we may begin to discern some of the valuable ways our difficulties serve us.

For instance, an illness or injury can provide a *gateway to transformation*, as was the case with Joanna and her family due to her sprained ankle. Her injury effectively nullified her habitual role in her parents' relationship and, along with the pressure provided by the mother's terminal illness, created an opportunity for the healing of that relationship. Gary's knee gave him the time and opportunity to explore a painful aspect of his life, the first step in beginning to heal it. Darren, diagnosed as having AIDS, changed both his lifestyle and his values as a result of that diagnosis. His grandmother was changed as well, into a condition of greater love and compassion.

Second, an illness or injury may be chosen by the soul not only to heal some aspect of the individual's consciousness, but to heal an aspect of the greater group consciousness as well. When this occurs what is operating is known esoterically as the *law of sacrifice*. Whenever the well-being or the consciousness of the many is advanced by the suffering of the few, the law of sacrifice is operating. Darren's illness is certainly a demonstration of this law in operation. I believe every person stricken with AIDS can be seen from this perspective, seen as part of a great group of souls dedicated in this incarnation to expressing the law of sacrifice, suffering in order that the consciousness of humanity may be advanced.

A third way that illness, injury, or physical distress may serve us occurs when we are attempting to ignore distressing conditions in our lives by being less than honest with ourselves. The body's problems can serve as an *indicator of our psychological evasions*. Every difficult situation in life is a test, and as we evolve so do our tests, from situations that challenge our physical courage to those that try our moral courage, our personal integrity, and our capacity for self-honesty. None of these tests is easy. Because we would ignore or avoid them if we could, the body's distress serves two purposes. It alerts us that an issue exists that demands to be addressed, and it makes the consequences of our attempts to deny this fact sufficiently painful that our temporizing becomes too costly. Through the very symptoms it manifests, the body can point up whatever we're trying to deny.

The body and the personality in conflict

The body is a wondrous thing, the animal part of us with its own animal brain—and it's own animal instincts and emotions. Like any other animal, *the human body is incapable of dishonesty*. This simple fact causes us human beings no end of problems. Actually the problems don't arise so much from the inability of the body to lie as from the personality's all too well developed capacity to do so. Self-conscious and self-evaluating, we try to convince ourselves that what we've decided we should be is what, indeed, we are. Meanwhile, the physical body goes right on reacting with no judgments whatsoever, all pure instinct and emotion, embarrassing us thoroughly in the process. It blushes, it blanches, its pupils dilate, teeth chatter, jaws clench, palms sweat. It humiliates us with an untimely erection or fails us by trembling or fainting—heedlessly exposing to all the world our sexual arousal, our fear, our embarrassment or anger or whatever reaction the thinking, judging, *human* part of us is trying so hard to hide.

What happens when our physical body is experiencing and expressing one state of being while the human ego, with its desire to meet with its own and others' approval, is bent on expressing another?

Our physical body exists in the physical dimension and is nourished by matter—air, water, food—from the physical plane. Our astral and mental bodies exist on the astral or mental plane and are nourished through their chakras by astral or mental matter from their respective plane.

When each of these bodies, physical and subtle, is clear and free of distortion, the vibration of the entire human energy field or aura will also be clear and even. Physical problems create distortions in the aura and so do problems in the subtle bodies. When distortion is present in the subtle bodies, the flow of energy through the chakras to these bodies may be blocked. Prolonged distortion or dissonance is advanced as a cause of disease by those who are able through highly developed clairvoyance to observe the workings of the body at these subtler energetic levels. Brief but severe episodes of dissonance can contribute to passing ills such as indigestion, headaches, colds, the flu. More prolonged and habitual distortions in the field can predispose the body to far more serious diseases such as cancer.

Dishonesty and dissonance

Here are a few examples of how the body's condition can signal that we are ignoring a source of emotional or mental stress.

One young woman came into the chiropractor's office barely able to lift her head because of excruciating pain that radiated through the back of her neck and both shoulders. She had just returned from a visit with her mother, during which the mother was hospitalized due to heart pain. This emergency was triggered when she neglected to take her daily heart medication during her daughter's visit. The daughter described the situation this way:

"Sometimes I feel as though I've been carrying my mother forever. It's her life, but she won't take responsibility for it. She never has. Now what am I supposed to do, move back down there to make sure she takes her pills every day?"

This young woman had recently begun work she very much enjoyed and had started a promising new romance as well. The prospect of returning to her role as her mother's caretaker was unbearable, as was the idea that her mother might die unless she did so. Both the chiropractor and I recognized that the heavy yoke of pain across her shoulders and neck perfectly correlated with the emotional burden she felt. As we helped her acknowledge her deep resentment of her mother's manipulative helplessness and accept that she needed to release her mother to her own fate, the pain began to recede.

Frequently, as in the case below, I saw the chiropractor working to ease a condition that the body had created in order to alert the patient to an intolerable situation, whether at home or at work.

A woman came in complaining of a recent onslaught of headaches and digestive disturbances. She chatted away nonchalantly about the following situation: She had rented a room in her house to a man with whom she had had a brief affair, hoping they would continue to be romantically involved. However, once he was in the house there were no further romantic overtures forthcoming. In fact, he soon became involved with another woman with whom he had long conversations on the telephone he shared with his landlady, our patient. She described these calls as "rude" and "thoughtless," but when asked if she felt angry and wanted to ask him to move out, she replied, "Oh, no. I wouldn't *think* of it. We're all adults. I could *never* be a jealous person!"

I remember thinking that I wasn't convinced and neither apparently was her body, since the onset of her symptoms coincided with the onset of his new affair, and she suffered principally during the evenings when he conducted his lengthy telephone tête-à-têtes. Her efforts not to think about what was happening right in front of her may well have brought about the evening headaches, and since the gallbladder and its secretion of bile are historically associated with envy and jealousy, that may explain the source of her digestive problems. Unless she could heed her body's warning about this living situation, it was likely her symptoms would continue.

Certainly not every physical ailment has a psychological cause. But many do, and when that is the case often, as with Gary and with this woman, we want the body "fixed," the pain relieved through medical help—drugs, surgery, hypnosis, acupuncture, or other approaches—because we won't acknowledge that the deeper, nonphysical source of the pain needs addressing. To ignore or deny such a nonphysical source may be to ultimately court the development of even more serious physical problems.

This was the case with Karen, a woman who attended a workshop on healing through the energy field. One of our tasks as participants was to discover the ways we were ignoring signals from the body that indicated areas of dishonesty in our lives.

Another task was to awaken higher powers of perception, so that we could in some way sense the energetic configurations of these distortions. From my years of study, I had already become aware of perceiving subtler dimensions of reality. I had learned to pay attention when I got strong emotional "hits" from a place or person or a name. I could sometimes pick up the energies from objects and tell the story connected with them, and looking at someone's photograph often opened a window into that person's inner being for me. Occasionally I saw configurations and colors in a person's energy field that indicated strongly held beliefs or feelings or conflicts.

At the end of our time together, we were describing what we

had gained from our experience. Karen, who was in her early thirties, was at the time in remission from cancer of the throat. She had struggled for years to make her mark as an actress. During a particularly dry spell in her career, she had married and later had complied with her husband's desire for a family. Ever since, she had been struggling to fit her acting jobs around her family obligations and often felt torn between her devotion to her husband and children and her great love, the theater. Now, in a burst of optimistic virtue, she told us she was going to put her acting aside, go home, and rededicate herself to her husband and children and to the happiness of her family. I watched aghast as her energy field responded to what she was saying. A dark, somber, stiff, and heavy gray-green mantle enveloped her as she spoke, and I realized with a shock that she was possibly pronouncing her own death sentence. However praiseworthy her commitment to being a fine wife and mother sounded, it was not the honest direction for her to be taking and her emotional body knew it. Because energy follows thought, this mantle of astral matter was created to match the restriction her plan actually represented for her. Perhaps she felt she had no choice, caught as she must have been between her need to live a responsible, respectable life and that deeper desire of her heart—acting on the stage. Her choice to put her family first may not even have been the wrong one given her value system. It simply wasn't the most *honest* one, and I could see from her energy field how she really felt.

What might her energy field have shown had she announced instead a decision to follow her heart, whatever that meant? Her aura would have been more highly charged and more brightly colored. Though the conflicts she felt regarding her family would still have been represented in her field, she would have had more energy with which to cope. Instead, she was wrapping herself in the mantle of "good wife and mother," a mantle that, for her, was dangerously stifling.

I don't pretend to know what the answer would have been for Karen. I do know that she was making a choice that would serve to depress her overall energy field and thus her immune system, not something a cancer patient can readily afford. Although it might seem that her body was betraying her with cancer, wasn't it possible that by ignoring her true interests, she was betraying her body?

How the body serves the soul

Which is better? For Karen to wholeheartedly pursue her acting? Or to give it up and devote herself to her family, though her body may not be able to survive her choice? Life, our life, the life we've chosen and designed from the far greater wisdom and perspective of the soul, does that to us. It slams us into a corner, makes the stakes very, very high, as high as life and death, love and respect, our beloved children or the calling of our heart—then forces us to choose. And what do we have to guide us in our choice? On the one hand there is the pressure of society's standards and our own, shaped as they are by necessity and the times in which we live. On the other hand our heart exhorts us: "This above all things: to thine own self be true."

This testing is the very essence of Earth-plane existence. Called "fire by friction" by the esotericists, these predicaments and dilemmas, through the pressures they create, abrade our rough spots and leave us finally pure and shining, though not necessarily in one lifetime. It is a long, long process, and while we are in its throes we are rarely appreciative of its refining effects. All we know is that we're suffering and we envy those who aren't, believing them to be somehow living more correctly than we are and therefore to be more blessed. Don't we, both individually and as a society, tend to give greater spiritual credit to those whose lives are neat and orderly, believing them to be better than those of us who are struggling with our assorted afflictions?

We would be closer to the truth of the situation if we remembered that life on this Earth plane is a classroom and that as one advances through school the tasks become more complicated. Every grade is necessary to our ultimate development. Each is challenging when we are at that level, but as soon as we have mastered one level we must go on to the next. None of us, having learned what second grade has to teach us, would want to stay there forever. Instead, we eagerly embrace our next course of study. Later, in the midst of a new challenge, we forget the choice was ours.

Perhaps the body is more attuned to our choices than we are. It rebels when we stray too far from what is right for us. And it pays a price for the stress our choices engender. In doing what we ask of it, and paradoxically even in rebelling, the body is the servant of the soul.

I learned a new way of relating to my body when I failed to regain mobility after knee surgery. Because the recommended exercises were not helping, I decided instead to approach my body as I would my beloved horse—gently, kindly, reassuringly. I stopped every kind of treatment that was painful, let go of my anger and impatience that my body wasn't yet performing as I wished, and touched it only with love. All this required constant discipline as I had always taken my body for granted, often forcing it to do what I wanted even when it responded with pain. As I learned a new respect and appreciation for both my body and for what my injury was teaching me, my knee slowly began to heal.

In Nikos Kazantzakis's book *Saint Francis*, the saint regards the physical body as a willing pack animal that nevertheless has needs of its own. When his companion, Leo, is ashamed to admit his hunger, Francis gently encourages him to eat, saying, "Feed your donkey."

Yes, feed your donkey with proper food and rest. Treat it with respect. Offer it love and gratitude for all the ways it serves you. And remember to listen to its wisdom.

Three

Is There a Bigger Picture I'm Not Seeing?

D id you ever, as a child, work on a picture in a paint-by-numbers kit? Do you remember filling in each tiny outlined space with the color designated by the number in that space? Perhaps all spaces with a three were to be filled with orange. You looked at the picture on the front of the kit to see what that area was supposed to look like and maybe it was the shadow of a tree. You thought "No, that can't be right. Shadows are gray or black or maybe even deep blue or purple, but never orange!" Yet the space had a three in it and a three meant orange, so you filled it in, certain a mistake had been made. You worked along conscientiously, but even after you'd filled in many spaces you couldn't discern a picture, only random dots of color. And then, as you continued to paint, those tiny random dots magically sorted themselves into highlights and shadings. Finally, images emerged to form a meaningful picture, with points of light in areas of shadow and traces of darkness in areas of light. Now you no longer noticed the individual spaces because the overall effect obliterated the details.

Each individual lifetime is much like that—an unfolding mon-
tage of events, emotions, and thoughts all having their own
quality or color. Taken together these bits and pieces form the
meaningful design that is this life we're living. The design cannot
be readily seen, however, while we're busily living it. A client once
demanded, "How can you *see* your life when you're *in* it?" She
posed as a figure frozen in a painting, then craned her neck
straining to see, across a flat plane, the overall composition of
which she was a part. Seeing the whole picture was, of course,
impossible.

This lack of perspective, of distance from the events in our lives
forces us to guess as we go along about their possible meaning
and value. Usually we base our evaluation of whatever is occurring
on how we *feel* when it is happening—comfortable or uncomfortable, satisfied or dissatisfied, happy or depressed. When the life
we're leading is unfolding the way we anticipated, we assume
we're doing things correctly. If there are disturbing events and
feelings we hadn't expected, we think "No, this can't be right. I'm
not supposed to be living this way. There must be a mistake."
Sometimes, reflecting on past troubles, we are able to see how
they helped us develop our current level of understanding and
self-awareness. Or their meaning may still be hidden from us in
a wider context that may even include other lifetimes.

A case of sexual addiction

Jerry, in his early thirties and already twice divorced, was at
home in the apartment where he lived alone. He was battling a particularly virulent strain of flu while the company

he worked for was undergoing a corporate takeover. When Jerry wasn't too overcome by fever, he worried about being overlooked during the reorganization that was going on in his absence. He kept the television playing day and night to distract him from his worries about work and about women.

His most recent romance had ended disastrously when the latest in his string of young girlfriends under twenty refused to see him after he was repeatedly impotent during lovemaking. Though by no means the first such failure, it hadn't yet happened so early in a relationship. He was getting scared. He had always before been able to put the blame for his failure on his partner. He told himself it was something she had said or done or that he wasn't attracted to her after all, but his rationalizations weren't working so well anymore. He found himself relying solely on fantasy to be able to perform at all. He could not tolerate his partner speaking or in any other way distracting him during the sex act. And the girls featured in his fantasies were always faceless and getting younger and younger.

It was midafternoon when a television host announced a program on men as victims of incest. Annoyed, Jerry reached for the remote control to change the channel, forgetting that he had inadvertently carried it into the kitchen. Shivering with an onslaught of chills, he gave up the search and buried himself in the bed covers, while on television a psychotherapist described the frequency with which boys are sexually abused by members of their own family. The therapist correlated these experiences with later problems with intimacy and sexual functioning. Too weak to get out of bed, Jerry found himself increasingly annoyed with the program.

Meanwhile, a man appearing on the screen in silhouette began to describe his own rape at the age of ten by a drunken older brother and his inability throughout his life to associate feelings of love with the sex act. He talked about his addiction to pornography and his several failed marriages. Finally, Jerry dragged himself out of bed and across the room, reaching past the stacks of girlie magazines and sex videos on his dresser to turn the television off manually. He climbed back in bed, the room quiet now for the first time in all the days he'd been home ill. When he finally drifted off to sleep he dreamed of a young boy suffering what the man had described, but the boy was Jerry as a child and the perpetrator was the man in silhouette.

At the end of the week Jerry returned to work, not yet fully recovered but worried that staying away longer might mean the loss of his job. His stomach was still so queasy that he didn't dare follow his usual routine of heading for a bar after work. He especially missed alcohol's numbing effects because the dream of the boy and the silhouetted man seemed to be haunting him, flashing into his consciousness several times a day. Each time it again brought on chills and nausea.

On Saturday he met a young girl at the car wash and talked her into following him home in her own car. When he tried to make love to her, suddenly the vision was there again, ruining everything. While she dressed the girl was silent, but as she walked out of his apartment she remarked, not unkindly, that maybe he should think about getting some help. Instead Jerry, still unable to drink, assuaged his discomposure with a trip to an out-of-town adult bookstore.

That night, Jerry dreamed his dream again and suddenly, while the face of the boy was his own as a child, the perpetrator's face was also his, an aged version of his adult self. He awakened and poured himself a drink in spite of his nauseated condition. Meanwhile the vision persisted, accompanied by strong sexual feelings. He found himself fantasizing about having sex with a child, a quiet, compliant child who wouldn't know or care about his impotence. Then, as all the sexual feelings drained away, Jerry was in the bathroom vomiting and vomiting and vomiting.

He didn't dare sleep again after that, unwilling to risk the direction his dreams might take. The thought that he couldn't soothe himself with either sex or alcohol panicked him. Long comfortless hours later when the sun finally came up, Jerry was willing to consider getting help. A sympathetic coworker had recommended a therapist to him after his last divorce, and Jerry put in a call, half hoping that because it was Sunday there would be no answer. When the answering service gave him an appointment for the following evening, he consoled himself with the thought that if the therapist didn't help, then maybe he could kill himself. It wasn't an altogether new idea.

During their first appointment the therapist, through careful questioning, discerned that Jerry was in trouble with alcohol and made abstinence a condition of therapy. Jerry, surprised at his response of relief, agreed.

By his second session Jerry trusted the therapist enough to be able to describe the vision that was haunting him. Within a few sessions he had admitted his obsession with sexual fantasies and his need for ever younger and more anonymous partners. At his therapist's suggestion he began attending meetings of a twelve-step program for those addicted to sex. There he got the support he needed in order not to act out his sexual addiction.

Meanwhile, in therapy he was piecing together his own suppressed and denied early history of sexual abuse. It had occurred over a period of many months at the hands of his father's brother, recently returned from Vietnam and living in Jerry's family home. This uncle, who never recovered emotionally after taking part in the war, subsequently moved from Jerry's home to a boarding house, where within months he shot himself to death. A significant portion of Jerry's trauma was connected to his uncle's violent death, a death he as a child was certain he had brought about through wishing so ardently for it.

Remembering and reliving the experiences from that most difficult time took all of Jerry's courage and perseverance. He was finally bringing out of exile the linked portions of his physical, emotional, and mental bodies that had been ravaged by his uncle's assaults so many years before and that had been energetically frozen and anesthetized ever since. Jerry needed to *remember* and *reincorporate* these frozen and rejected parts of himself and his experience.

It is interesting to note that the roots of both *remember* and *incorporate* refer to the body: *member* to the limbs and *corpus* to the body itself. To re-member is to reattach a body part that has been lost or detached; to re-incorporate is to take back into the body a part that has been left outside or rejected. The common usage of both these words indicates that the processes of forgetting or disowning affect us in a physical way. Something vital to the physical body's functioning is lost or distorted. I would suggest that this effect is precipitated by damage in the subtler mental and emotional bodies where energetic freezing, blocking, and dissonance occurs. Damage to these subtler bodies must be addressed in order to restore healthy physical functioning. As Jerry was able to allow the disowned parts of himself—his experiences and related emotions and thoughts—back into consciousness, their power to cripple and corrupt began to diminish.

The roots of victimization in the past

Think of Jerry for a moment as the adult who was, prior to beginning therapy, becoming progressively more dependent on impersonal sexual experiences, in need of explicit magazines and videos and fantasy for stimulation, requiring ever younger partners for ever more anonymous encounters, edging toward a pattern of compulsion and perversion.

Then think of little four-year-old Jerry sexually abused by his deeply disturbed uncle.

It may feel as though you are thinking about two very separate people, an innocent child who evokes your sympathy and a responsible adult toward whom you feel aversion. And Jerry, in recovery, is *yet* another person, courageously struggling to acknowledge his sexual exploitation as a child and admit his sexually exploitive behavior as an adult.

Already we can see that there have been several Jerrys in one lifetime, each contributing to the unfolding and development of the next. Recognizing this, can you imagine Jerry's existence in other historical periods and other physical bodies? Place the essential being that is now Jerry on a continuum that spans numerous lifetimes as both male and female, that includes among many others the roles of victim and victimizer as well as the role of one who learns from incorporating both the victim's and the victimizer's experiences—do this and watch how your emotions regarding the various Jerrys gradually neutralize. A judgmental response toward the adult Jerry and a pitying attitude toward Jerry the child both give way to an appreciation of the larger picture. From this detached perspective it is possible to begin to understand why Jerry as an innocent child should have had to suffer the sexual trauma he did.

The evolution of human consciousness

We incarnate on the Earth plane in order to expand our consciousness. This takes place through many experiences over many lifetimes. The fact is, we all suffer sexual and every other kind of abuse at some point in our own evolutionary unfoldment—and we each in turn inflict all those same abuses. It is eventually necessary for each of us, in the development of our own consciousness, to experience *everything*. Our long series of physical incarnations doesn't begin with an evolved consciousness dedicated to the highest human principles. We must forge our way through many incarnations before the body and the personality finally become the willing, disciplined tools of the higher mind or soul—before we can consciously employ them to help our fellow human beings.

The journey is a long one. At the beginning, our animal instincts, urges, and appetites rule our existence. Though we may inflict great harm at this early stage, we are not yet truly capable of evil any more than a lion stalking its prey. We, like the lion, are still simply following our animal nature. But as we gather greater experience we learn, we grow, our consciousness develops and so does our *capacity to choose*.

In a spiritual sense the greatest distinction between the animal kingdom and ours is our far greater and ever-evolving capacity for conscious choice. This capacity is not, however, equally evolved and developed among all the members of the human race at the same time. We begin our evolutionary cycle at different times and progress at differing rates. But until each of us is sufficiently advanced, our body's instincts and promptings, like those of the animals, will make many of our choices for us.

I once had a client whose impulsive and aggressive behavior had already led to problems with the law. He was now headed for prison. This time, while drinking in a bar, he had shoved another man who fell, hit his head, and died. My young client had far more brute strength than his primitive emotions and undeveloped intellect could safely handle. Free of guile but utterly under the sway of physical appetites and emotional impulses, he was clearly what is known as a "young soul," struggling to learn the most basic principles of self-control. Even though his actions resulted in another's death, he, like Steinbeck's Lenny in *Of Mice and Men*, radiated not evil but a kind of hapless, childlike innocence.

We all begin as "young souls," with our journey into full human consciousness stretching far ahead of us. Esoterically we are, at this early stage, known as "infant humanity." Like children we are

in the early stages of physical, emotional, and mental development. Like them, too, our early explorations of the physical world
are limited chiefly by the degree of pain we are able to tolerate in
our own body. Our capacity for empathy eventually develops
through long eons of suffering and inflicting suffering in turn.
Until that capacity develops, we are only restrained from harming
others by the possibility of punishment. As with maturing children, we must evolve in consciousness before the restraints on
our behavior are internal rather than external.

One of the reasons children, unless restrained or carefully
taught otherwise, often behave cruelly toward one another and
toward animals and insects is that they are progressing through
one of the early developmental stages of their own evolution of
consciousness. What seems to an adult's matured consciousness
to be an expression of cruelty is often in many children simply
curiosity, untempered by compassion. It is interesting to note
that John Muir and Joseph Wood Krutch, both great naturalists,
report in their autobiographies that as children they often treated
animals with cruelty.

By the age of twenty-one we have usually matured sufficiently
to express whatever level of consciousness the experiences of
prior lifetimes have imparted. This level of consciousness varies
greatly from one individual to another depending on what has
already been accomplished during previous incarnations. For
instance, an individual's regard for the physical, emotional, and
mental sovereignty of another human being cannot simply be
inculcated through education stressing humanitarian concepts.
Even the word *education* is derived from *educere*, meaning to draw
forth something that is already there. Unless the person has al-

ready achieved the capacity for such respect through the experiences of other lifetimes, education cannot elicit it.

How we design an incarnation

Any given incarnation has its roots in all that has gone before but most especially in the episode of Earth life just previous. Throughout our countless early incarnations, the chief purpose of our existence here is the amassing of physical-plane experience. Later, we undertake incarnations in order to understand and, when necessary, heal that which has been experienced.

A review of the life just completed takes place each time we leave the physical body in death. This life review has been described by many who have undergone near-death experiences as an objective review free of the personality's dictates. From it we are able to identify, with the help of our Guides, who are usually our own completed incarnations acting under the direction of our soul, what we most need to address next. We are helped to isolate the *three major conditioning factors* that will define the essence of our coming incarnation. We set up the circumstances necessary to our next assignment and conceive the design of our physical, astral, and mental vehicles with which to accomplish it. This is analogous to deciding at the end of one school year which courses we should pursue when we return to our studies and then making sure we have the proper equipment to do so.

The first of the conditioning factors is the *nature of the physical environment* in which we will next incarnate. All of us recognize that the general culture, the particular social milieu, and the status, interests, and pursuits of the family into which we are born all powerfully shape our development. If we understand that this field of experience is *chosen* prior to incarnation because it provides the background we require for the tasks we have set ourselves, we realize we have been neither victimized nor exalted by Fate. Rather, we are in the midst of what we require to pursue our incarnational goals.

The second determining factor is *the degree of refinement and the strengths and weaknesses of the physical body.* It is taught esoterically that the most karmic factor in any incarnation is the physical body, and the most karmic part of the physical body is its nervous system. We choose the body that best suits the work of each lifetime. Our particular nervous system, by interpreting the world for us in its own characteristic way, profoundly structures our every experience and thus our overall view of life. And our natural abilities determine our path of least resistance, causing us to emphasize the activities and interests that come easily while our weaknesses preclude other endeavors.

The third factor is the *makeup of the astral or emotional body,* which determines to what and to whom we are attracted and, in turn, who and what we attract. This emotional body is linked to our perceptions of the world around us through our nervous system. Our physical senses of touch, taste, smell, hearing, and sight interpret the environment in a manner conditioned and flavored by the emotional body.

And just as our emotional body affects, via the nervous system, how we experience every dimension of the environment, so the environment is, in turn, affected by every dimension of our entire being. Whether we are conscious of the fact or not, we human beings perceive one another as complete energy packages. Every level in our aura, every one of our subtle bodies responds to the corresponding energetic dimension in another person. And these responses are emotional. Through the attractions governed by our emotional body we seek out and are sought by those with whom we have business to attend to in a given lifetime, or perhaps in lifetime after lifetime—those in our karmic group. This group may or may not include our family of origin, but it always includes those with whom we have important and life-changing associations.

The exercise of free will

Thus we come into physical-plane existence with what might be referred to as an agenda for which we are primed through previous experiences in previous existences. This agenda is expressed by our environment and by our physical, emotional, and mental equipment. Indeed, it is during the period between incarnations that we most truly exercise our free will, for it is then that we determine, with the help of our Guides, the conditions and areas of emphasis for our next sojourn on Earth. Throughout a given lifetime each of our available choices exists within these previously determined parameters, which are in turn a result of our past incarnational history. We must ever work with what we have been as we evolve into that which we yearn to become.

Morphogenetic resonance and healing cycles

When it is time for us to return to the Earth plane, the soul assembles our mental and emotional bodies for the coming incarnation from matter expressing the vibratory gradations present in those bodies at the close of the last incarnation. Because it is rare indeed that we don't learn something from each sojourn here and because we always carry forward every gain, it is guaranteed that we *evolve* rather than *devolve*. Whatever was improved has its energetic component in these emotional and mental bodies, as does whatever remained blocked or distorted at the time of death. Again the situation is analogous to school. Everything we have already learned is now automatically a part of us and we must focus on what we need to learn next. We literally embody our next lessons, because whatever needs to be healed from the past will have its energetic equivalent in one or another of our bodies in the present. Further, *whatever is still distorted in us attracts more of the same.* This occurs because like fields of energy are attracted to one another through a principle described by Rupert Sheldrake as *morphogenetic resonance.*

Another way of saying this is that we attract our karma and our karma attracts us. Automatically, those people, those events, and those circumstances that match or mirror our own distortions are drawn to our energy field and thus shape our life experience and relationships. Through these transactions, called *healing cycles*, we are given the opportunity to get better or, if we resist our life experience, to get worse.

How healing cycles work

Whether we get better or worse, every such transaction is a healing cycle because it moves us through our distortion. Even entering more deeply into our distortion makes our eventual surrender and emergence through healing more likely.

In Jerry's case, every new attempt at a physical relationship initiated another healing cycle because each failure made it all the more likely that eventually he would have to surrender and begin the healing process. Actually, Jerry had no choice about whether or not he would heal, only about *when*.

This is true for all of us. Our lives while incarnate are like a train on a track. We can decide when to stop and where and for how long. We can even decide to back up. But the direction our journey will take is fixed. The only real question is how quickly we'll reach our destination.

Resisting our healing is one of the very few significant free-will choices we have while incarnate. As long as we resist, the distortion or blockage grows because it accrues more and more energy attached to more and more experience. Eventually (this may take lifetimes and often does, but then, the soul has all of eternity) the very weight or mass of the distortion brings to bear sufficient pressure to force a change. We are finally exhausted and defeated by our obsession with money, property, power, fame, pride, vanity, our righteousness, our victimization, or whatever. Collapsing under the pressure of our obsession or illusion we are, like Jerry, paradoxically restored to wholeness as we surrender in defeat.

False gods and healing cycles

The biblical injunction, "Thou shalt have no other gods before me," refers to our relationship with our soul. Whatever gets in the way of that relationship, whatever we worship in its place is a false god, an image we have usually carried over from lifetime to lifetime that has led us away from our higher nature and therefore must eventually be destroyed.

Paul had a vineyard, a magnificent stretch of sunny, protected land that fronted on a peaceful inlet and rose to
rounded hills overlooking the sea. There was a graceful
home, the country house in which he had spent the happiest
days of his childhood. Alone there with his mother and the
household help, Paul was glad when his father stayed in the
city, only arriving at the house on an occasional weekend
during those long, sweet summers.

There was no beach like that beloved beach, no earth like
that from which the vines grew, no view like the one from
those soft hills, no house in all the world so pleasant and
light and airy and full of sweet memories as that one, long
since converted to his year-round home.

And now he was losing it all. By nature much more like
his gentle, dreamy, soft-spoken mother than his hard-driving,
despotic father, Paul had no head for business. He was impulsive rather than shrewd, and in his hands after his father's
death, the considerable fortune he'd inherited diminished
and finally disappeared. He'd mortgaged the vineyard as a
stopgap measure, then found he had to mortgage it further,
risking the only thing he couldn't bear losing. A year ago the
property had gone into foreclosure. Only through borrowed
money and on borrowed time was he still living in the place
he loved most on earth.

There had been three wives but only one son, Phillip,
who had been told all his life that the vineyard would be his
someday. Paul never seemed to notice that Phillip didn't
share his love for the house or the land, that crowded cities
full of fast-talking, fast-moving people appealed to him far
more than an empty stretch of beach or rows and rows of

disciplined vines heavy with magenta grapes. After Phillip, a canny businessman like his grandfather, had made a considerable fortune of his own, Paul was stunned to learn his son wouldn't help save the property.

Though Paul couldn't acknowledge this fact, it wasn't his love for Phillip that created his yearning to pass the vineyard on to him. Rather, Paul's love for the vineyard rendered Phillip all the more important as its heir. Now Paul had been living for years under the threat of losing his beloved land because of his son's indifference to his inheritance and, it would seem, to his father as well. Without money for upkeep, the house's charm was fading and the vineyard had deteriorated into a sad tangle of weeds. One week before he was to vacate the premises in order to make way for the new owners, Paul suffered a nearly fatal heart attack.

In the hospital, when Phillip visited, Paul expressed little interest in living now that everything that ever mattered to him was gone. Bitterly, he blamed the loss of the property on his son's selfishness, to which Phillip replied coldly, "You loved that land way too much, Dad, more than anything or anybody else."

Paul survived a necessary surgery, slowly recovered and eventually married his fourth wife, Sally, an energetic and cheerful woman who, unlike his previous wives, didn't have to compete with the vineyard for his love and attention. Sally coped easily with Paul's impractical nature; she helped him sort out his remaining assets, encouraged him to become more businesslike in his financial affairs, and gently urged a reconciliation between him and Phillip.

It took Paul many years to overcome his bitterness toward

his son. But finally, in his late seventies, he met with Phillip to acknowledge the truth of his son's accusation.

"You were right," he admitted. "I loved that land too much. God knows it was beautiful but I always put it first. I would have sacrificed everything and everybody just to hang onto it. In fact, I guess that's exactly what I did—and I'm sorry."

Not surprisingly, Phillip now has two grown sons who mystify him with their complete indifference to the world of business and finance. Instead they are dedicated to a joint venture in organic farming that produces so little income they are just barely scratching along. Phillip lectures them about the kind of return they could expect for their hours of work in some other line of business, but they don't listen. Somehow his visits with them on the farm seem to go better when he takes their grandfather Paul and Sally along. . . .

Paul was born into a male line of descent where an attachment to money alternated with an attachment to property in taking precedence over human relationships. It is interesting to note the incremental changes in this attitude as the generations proceeded, as well as how each generation played off those that went before and followed. Obviously Paul's story is an example of the strong factor our field of experience can be in providing us with the opportunity to confront our lessons.

How we attract our lessons from
the environment

Sometimes our lessons come as much or more from the work our emotional body does in attracting to us, out of a vast sea of strangers, precisely those people and situations we need to help move us through our distortions.

Ardath's story illustrates the principle of attraction between like distortions and demonstrates how healing cycles work. She, like Jerry, was an incest victim, abused by her step-father over a ten-year period. Unlike Jerry, however, she had not been able to repress the memory of her abuse but had lived with it daily right into her thirty-fifth year, when she finally decided to go into therapy. She chose a minister who specialized in treating adults with "trust issues."

The minister/therapist frequently required that his clients, while relating incidents of trauma from their childhoods, lie on the floor blindfolded and accept being touched and held by him. Though this was supposedly an exercise in trust building, in Ardath's case what grew instead were her feelings of uneasiness. The minister repeatedly assured her that although it would take time, there would be a breakthrough if she persevered. A breakthrough did indeed occur one day when, squirming with discomfort, she suddenly pulled the blindfold off and saw the minister standing over her, masturbating. Ardath's shocked revulsion was intense. Through his mumbled explanations and excuses she fled the office in a blizzard of emotion. Within days a state of deep depression had completely overwhelmed her, accompanied by irrational guilt that she had somehow caused his behavior by agreeing to participate in the blindfold exercises.

Feeling doubly distrustful but nearly incapacitated by her depression, she finally sought help again, this time from a woman therapist. Her new counselor, recognizing the rage beneath Ardath's depression, urged her to prosecute. With the new therapist's support, Ardath brought steady pressure to bear for nearly two years on the deputy district attorney in charge of the case. Although several other women had come forward to tell stories similar to Ardath's, he was reluctant to prosecute with only one victim—Ardath—willing to testify. But Ardath wouldn't give up, wouldn't let the case die, wouldn't remain silent.

Finally the case was brought to court and the minister immediately pled guilty. It was over. She'd won the battle fought on behalf of the little girl she had been, the little girl to whom no one would listen, whom no one believed, who'd had no champion through all those years of abuse. She had grown up to become her own advocate and had thereby healed herself.

A final footnote to this story: some months before Ardath's shocking discovery, I heard this man's voice on an answering machine when I tried to return his call regarding a business matter. His voice is still unforgettable to me, sinister and seductive at the same time. Yet Ardath, and several other women, trusted him enough to do as he bid them, including lying blindfolded on the floor at his feet. Why? Why were they unaware of his obviously untrustworthy character? *Because they were initiating another healing cycle.* Remember that we get worse until we get better, that we go deeper into the problem in order to finally surrender to healing it, whatever that may mean.

Jerry's surrender made him willing to reveal his secret, made seeing a therapist possible, which in turn led him to acknowledge his history of abuse and start practicing a twelve-step program of recovery. Paul had to lose what he loved most—his property—before he could recognize what his obsession had cost him in human relationships. And when Ardath finally surrendered her passive role in her own victimization, her healing cycle took her to the next necessary step, championing her own cause and becoming an advocate of the child she had been. It would be safe to assume in each case the issues addressed by these healing cycles reached back into past lifetimes.

Healing cycles reintroduce unresolved issues from other lifetimes again and again until the breakthrough occurs. When the awareness is complete, further healing cycles along a particular line are no longer necessary. (Interestingly, our Guides are often those people we were in a lifetime during which an especially significant healing cycle was achieved.)

The physics of karma

Some of the mystery about how we set up or initiate these necessary healing cycles was forever clarified for me by another unforgettable experience a few years later.

Because we had some business to conduct, I was meeting two women for lunch at a fashionable seaside resort hotel. Together, we entered the elegant dining room and headed toward our table, which overlooked the harbor.

As we read the menu, one of the women, Darla, leaned toward us and whispered, "Girls! If you want to see the kind of man I *really* find attractive, he's it," and she inclined her head toward the busboy who had just poured our water. I hadn't noticed him earlier but now, as she pointed him out, I was shocked. My instant impression from his bulldog carriage, narrowed eyes, jutting jaw, and the curl of his lip was of a man who had a violent streak and quite possibly liked to humiliate women. All I could say in response was, "Really? Him? He looks kind of dangerous to me." Darla just smiled.

"Well," said Lonnie confidentially, "since we're talking about this, I'll tell you why I'm sitting here with my back to the view. See that man over there?" She indicated him with a glance over her shoulder, catching his eye briefly. Darla and I tried not to be obvious as we looked. "He's been staring at me since we walked in here." And sure enough, he was. This thickset middle-aged man wearing a beautifully tailored suit was leaning back in his chair with an unlit cigar clamped between his teeth, looking Lonnie over as though she were a Thoroughbred filly up for auction and he was about to make a bid. He, like Darla's busboy, had been completely invisible to me until he was pointed out. There was a definite energetic connection humming between this obviously wealthy and powerful man and the much younger Lonnie, who was now openly returning his stare. Meanwhile, as our water glasses were refilled by the busboy, the texture of the silent but sexually charged exchange between him and Darla was palpable.

Over lunch I learned quite a bit about these women. Both had grown up with alcoholic fathers who had sexually abused them. Lonnie's father had inherited considerable wealth, which eventually dwindled to nothing through his drinking and gambling. Darla's father, who had been physically violent as well as sexually abusive, was a prison guard whose wife had deserted him when Darla was an infant. He had remarried twice and both these women had been, as was Darla, very seductive types in behavior and dress. Dark-haired and voluptuous, she had a long history of brief involvements with men who were usually much younger than she and often either violent or sexually addictive or both. Darla had never married. Lonnie had been married twice, both times to rather passive men who were addicted to pornography and who had inherited money.

My experience at lunch with these two women was one of the most illuminating in a lifetime dedicated to understanding the principles of attraction. I had watched *morphogenetic resonance* (the principle described by Rupert Sheldrake in which like energies or vibrations attract) in action as clearly as I can ever hope to see it. Each of these women resonated with a certain vibration, one with greed, the other with violence, both with sexual addiction. They showed me how all of us unconsciously embrace our karma, choosing what our life experiences will be through what we invoke in our surroundings and what is, in turn, evoked within us. Lonnie somehow communicated to the tycoon across the room that she was indeed for sale to the highest bidder, although he was a little too aggressive to really be her type. And Darla alerted the busboy that her sexual aggression matched his own.

It was easy to see that Lonnie and Darla would repeat their patterns with men, getting deeper and deeper into trouble until the underlying issues were forced into consciousness. But through getting in deeper, they themselves would have much to answer for. In other words they would have, in the process, generated much karma. That karma, activated by morphogenetic resonance, would continue to produce ever more drastic healing cycles. Through this principle of like attracting like at an energetic level, we have a basic exposition of the physics of personal, family, and group karma in action.

Karma balances

Karma as a concept was widely introduced into Western thought with the upsurge of interest during the sixties in Eastern religions. The word suggests that a destiny is operating to balance the scales for past acts—including those from other lifetimes. We may refer to the concept of karma when faced with some otherwise inexplicable event, implying that if all were known there is a subtle justice being served. The fearful, retributive aspect of karma is frequently emphasized, is in fact many people's only definition of the word. This is not its essence, however. Karma is not a punitive or vindictive principle but a *balancing* one.

As we go about the necessary business of incarnation, which is to expand through various dimensions of experience, we create all kinds of effects, reactions, and repercussions. The Law of Karma ensures that balance accompanies all this activity and expansion. It is, therefore, in the widest sense, a law of healing of extremes and of restoration of balance. From our necessarily limited perspective, however, we may experience its implacable workings as harsh indeed. And if there weren't a key by which the endless process of generating more and more karma could be turned around, our situation would be one of devolution instead of evolution. We would become so mired in chain reactions that we could never hope for relief. Thankfully, the key does exist. It is *forgiveness*.

Forgiveness heals

To truly forgive requires that we truly understand. We must be able to look clearly at the whole picture, recoil from none of it, deny none of it, accept it all. In a way this means that we must become *experts* regarding that which we must forgive, seeing all sides, not just our own.

An example: I was in a workshop on the treatment of incest many years ago when, halfway through the morning, one of the participants identified himself as an aggressor who had sexually abused his daughter. For a long moment there was a stunned silence. Then he went on to describe his incarceration, the therapy he and his family had received, and his recovery of many years' duration. He now counseled male offenders incarcerated for the same offenses he had committed. With his wife and daughter, he participated in group discussions for the families of these men. His honesty created an environment that allowed other workshop participants to talk about their own experiences with sexual abuse. Because he modeled courage and dignity and humility as well as honesty, he made it easier for some of the therapists in the room who were also incest victims to gain more understanding of the person who had violated them. We stopped interacting as professionals and became *experts* instead, drawing on our *experience* as we struggled to understand this human problem. Such understanding, when achieved, leads eventually to forgiveness— and forgiveness is the final step in our healing. Through forgiving we are forgiven.

The phrase from the Lord's Prayer, ". . . forgive us our trespasses as we forgive those who trespass against us," takes on new meaning if we widen our perspective to include the many dimensions of ourselves expressed through many lifetimes. Remember Jerry the little boy, who was the victim, and Jerry the man, who was moving toward becoming the perpetrator. Surely both roles, trespasser and the person trespassed against, reside within us too, when we consider our evolution over many, many lifetimes. In order to heal completely we finally must acknowledge that we are not so very different from our enemy after all. And then, because our enemy represents that heretofore inadmissible part of ourselves, the part that we came here to heal, we must accept or love that enemy who has helped us to become reconciled with our self or soul.

George Stevens, the revered film director, said that when he was preparing to make the movie *The Diary of Anne Frank*, he first had to fully acknowledge the Nazi within himself. So must we all, every day, acknowledge the Nazi within us, and the murderer, the adulterer, the liar, the cheat, and the thief. Until we do we will encounter them outside ourselves again and again.

Our own resentment and bitterness, the hatred we feel toward our perceived enemy and the ways we wish that person ill, all comprise more potent configurations of evil than anything that takes place on the physical plane! If we are to be forgiven our trespasses we must forgive any trespasses against us. That is, we must *give* good *for* evil. *In the very act of forgiving*, our aura is cleansed, our vibration is raised.

In the New Testament we are told we must forgive not just once or even several times, but "seventy times seven." In other words, we must forgive endlessly and unstintingly. We may not yet consciously understand what debt we owe that makes our forgiveness necessary, but morphogenetic resonance—karma in action—guarantees we will draw to ourselves not only our lessons but our debts and the opportunity to pay them. And when they appear, how quickly and painlessly we discharge them depends so much on our attitude.

Years ago an event took place that I didn't understand at the time but that I now realize demonstrates the operation of mor-phogenetic resonance, healing cycles, and forgiveness. I was ad-dressing a largely female audience on the topic of relationship addiction. When I paused to ask for questions an attractive young woman, tall and blond, waved eagerly from the front row. At my nod she stood, addressing the entire room with her questions.

"What I want to know," she stated in a thoroughly charming Southern drawl, "is why I always attract *orphans*."

A little ripple of amusement ran through the audience and she frowned.

"Well, I do! Does anyone else here do that—attract orphans? Why, I've only been in this town a couple of days, and already I've met two, one at the airport and another in the lobby of my hotel. Honestly, I just seem to draw them to me like a magnet. How do I do that?"

It was an intriguing question and I certainly didn't have the answer. I knew nothing yet about morphogenetic resonance, but I did know that from my own early teens I had unconsciously attracted and been attracted to first boys and then men with serious alcohol and drug problems. After years of working as a therapist I recognized that many other women, too, consistently

attracted certain types of men who were troubled: violent men or
men who were chemically dependent or sexually compulsive or
workaholics. I even knew one woman who had unwittingly managed to marry two transvestites. So I was aware that many of us
were following patterns in our relationships, giving and receiving
subtle clues that caused us to choose and be chosen by certain
types of partners. But orphans?

"Were you adopted?" I asked her.

"No. Nothing like that. Perfectly ordinary family," she answered.

"Well, how do you feel about orphans?" I asked.

"Oh, I always just feel so *sorry* for them!" The drawl deepened.
"I feel that I've just got to help them, you know?"

I nodded.

"But still," she continued, "how do they know that about me?"
She looked around the audience again. "Do any of y'all have these
men who are orphans just coming up to you and introducing
themselves all the time?"

The entire audience shook their heads no, some of them
amused by her, others perplexed. Then they began firing questions.

"Do they look like they need your help?" someone near her
asked. She thought about it.

"Not usually. Some of them dress a lot better than I do," she
smilingly confessed.

"Do they tell you right away?" a voice from the back called out.

"No. It used to take longer, but now I've learned to ask early
on." The audience was buzzing.

"What about your girlfriends?" someone else called out.

"One of my two best girlfriends is an orphan," she said, so quietly that she had to repeat herself to be heard.

"Why do *you* think it happens?" a man behind her challenged.

"I wonder if it's something about the way I look. Can y'all see it?" She turned slowly, inviting their scrutiny. People looked hard but failed to catch whatever telltale sign she telegraphed to men who had, one way or another, lost their parents. Now she was looking at me again, her face questioning.

"I don't know. I don't see it," I told her, "but then, I'm not an orphan." There was another murmur of amusement. I asked my next question.

"What usually happens in these involvements?"

"Oh, we're friends for a while and then we finally just drift apart," she answered.

"No bad feelings? Bad experiences?"

"Oh, nooo!" She drew the word out for emphasis. "Never! Well, I mean, sometimes I loan them money or help them get a job or get on their feet, get started in school or whatever. Encourage them, you know? So maybe for a little while they lean on me." She looked around her. "But isn't that what y'all do, too? Try to help?"

From this audience made up largely of women who worked far too hard in their relationships with men, one woman quipped, "Yes. That's why we're here!"

The blond Southerner ducked her head, a little embarrassed. "Well, anyway, it's all friendly. And then"—she drew her hand gracefully through the air—"they just kind of fade out of my life. . . ."

She looked at me, shrugged her elaborate question all over

again, and when I shrugged my lack of an answer back, she sat down again.

Today I would guess that this woman was resolving some karmic debt with all those parentless persons who mysteriously appeared in her life. This would especially seem to be the case because she helped them so willingly, without expectation of emotional or financial return. Whatever the reason for these involvements, her story underlines the fact that significant human relationships are anything but random. We do not meet and engage with one another without assignable cause. Even when that cause is neither recognized nor understood, it is nevertheless operating as the balancing Law of Karma.

Forgiveness is the only "shortcut" through karma I've ever discovered. Through a simple willingness to forgive, our entire condition is raised up to a higher plane than that on which the Law of Karma operates. We enter a level where we no longer draw to ourselves more of the same difficulties and traumas through resonation. We enter the realm of Grace.

And so, as we go about the big and little tasks of each incarnation, painstakingly filling in space after space in the vast map of our evolutionary journey, it is love and forgiveness that finally suffuse our increasingly colorful canvas with pure white light.

Four

What Is the Point of the Pain?

was, as a young therapist in the field of addiction, sincerely dedicated to helping those alcoholics and addicts who were my clients, but I worked with only minimal success until I learned to require that all my addicted clients attend meetings of Alcoholics Anonymous or Narcotics Anonymous. Only then, with the understanding and support of others in recovery, could many of them stay clean and sober.

Still, professionally I did not come into my own until I left the alcoholics and addicts to the care of those in the appropriate anonymous program while I began to focus exclusively on working with their family members. I understood those spouses, parents, adult children, and others who loved someone who was addicted because I had shared their condition. I, too, had loved someone who was addicted. I had loved obsessively, as did so many of those who were now my clients, and I had learned how to recover from that wound by watching how those alcoholics who were my former clients were now recovering from their addiction in AA. I used the steps and methods they used (which include surrender to a Power higher than oneself and a strong emphasis on service), and their program began to work as well for my wound, my relationship addiction, as it did for their wound, their chemical dependency.

It's embarrassing to admit that I once actually believed that the alcoholics in my life were the source of all my problems! Today with gratitude I recognize each of those people as a catalytic agent for what still seems to me a miraculous recovery, addressing as it has so many of my deepest defects of character and correcting so much that was wrong with the way I interacted with other people. The years spent working with families and writing my two books on relationship addiction helped complete the healing cycle. They have been some of the most productive and fulfilling years of my life. And none of this would have been possible without the wound.

On the other hand, the years I spent in the throes of my co-alcoholic agony were excruciatingly painful. If someone had told me then that it was all necessary because I had so much to learn and this was the most efficient way for me to learn it . . . well, I'm not sure I would have been exactly grateful to hear that. And even though in retrospect I can see how necessary, even how perfect it all was, and that all the suffering was more than worth the gift, I still could not have consciously chosen to go through what I did in order to learn what I have. None of us would willingly go through the agonizing wounding in order to receive the gift, because the gift wouldn't seem worth the price from our unenlightened perspective.

Imagine someone appearing before you and saying, "You'll be going through quite a few difficulties during these next several years. You'll have ongoing depression that's intermittently crippling, and you'll completely collapse a couple of times with nervous breakdowns. You'll go through two divorces, lose both your children for a while because they won't be able to endure living with all your difficulties, and you'll develop severe food allergies and other health problems. Oh, and you'll be humiliated professionally when you are fired from your job. All this will bring you to your knees and you'll finally surrender enough to receive the help you need, not from a therapist but by taking a spiritual approach to your problems with the help of a support group of peers. Your recovery will take years but eventually you'll learn and understand much that you don't yet even realize is important. Then you'll truly be able to help other people in your practice and by writing books on relationship addiction."

What would your reaction be? All this and more happened to me, but if I'd been given the choice I would have said, "Forget it! Nothing's worth going through all that!"

And if, a few years later, I'd been informed ahead of time that in order to write this third book I'd have to first spend a very long and empty seven years in seclusion, I would have said, "No, I really couldn't do that. I'm much too active a person. There must be another way. . . ."

So you can see why the soul doesn't give us a choice. It knows what we need to experience and designs the physical, astral emotional, and mental bodies that together will make up our next vehicle for Earth-plane existence. These bodies cause us to attract those needed experiences without our conscious consent. The soul also knows that ultimately, though it may take many lifetimes, the lessons we've learned and the consciousness we've achieved will far outweigh the suffering we've endured. Besides, suffering either fades from memory the way labor pains usually do after a baby is born, or its lingering effects can be worked out later through healing cycles. But any advances in consciousness achieved during Earth-plane existence endure from incarnation to incarnation because they are stored in what is referred to esoterically as the "permanent atom," a dimension of our soul. They can be fairly easily restimulated once we've again reached sufficient physical, emotional, and mental maturity in a subsequent incarnation. This explains why so much of our subjective learning involves the "Aha!" experience. We are bringing back to consciousness some truth already stored deep within ourselves.

The evolutionary spiral

Consider the following as a formula for the soul's entire journey through Earth-plane existence, incarnating again and again into physical matter for the purpose of achieving expansion of consciousness:

Peace → Desire → Experience → Wound → Surrender
↑   ↓
Enlightenment ← Healing Gift ← Divine Intervention

All evolution happens in a spiral or cycle, and after each turn of the spiral there is a point of completion, a satiety that says "This is enough." Between incarnations, we have a resting period. Eventually that peace is once again stirred by the desire for expansion.

For human beings it is this desire that creates the pull toward every occasion of physical expression. The spiral winds upward until ultimate enlightenment provides the final release from the necessity for physical expression. Everything in between is experienced in order to contribute toward that enlightenment. This formula applies to the entire journey undertaken by each of us on behalf of the soul and begun long eons ago when the soul first answered the call to send a portion of itself down into physical matter for the purpose of the following:

EXPRESSION · EXPERIENCE · EXPANSION

The formula also applies to any *episode* of expression, experience, and expansion within that greater journey. An episode may take place entirely within one lifetime or extend over many before the awareness leading to healing through understanding and remediation is attained.

What is your wound?

The fact that you are reading this book very likely means that, in terms of the formula for the evolution of consciousness, you are involved in an episode at the point of the wound and are struggling to free yourself of its pain. In this context a wound is any condition that causes us deep and long-lasting emotional distress, whether or not our condition would affect another person the same way. Our wound may be based on internal or external factors; it may be inflicted on us by others or by Fate; it may be a permanent condition or one that will eventually diminish or cease to be a burden. Whatever its nature, we almost always feel that our wound is unfair and undeserved. Finally, as we will see, a wound is experienced very differently at different stages in our healing. What was at one point considered a confining prison later becomes a gateway into realization.

So now let's take a look at your wound and the ways it is working in your life and on your consciousness. We are not trying to "fix" it because fixing wounds isn't our true goal—expansion of consciousness is. However, greater understanding expedites the process of healing and expansion.

It might be a helpful exercise if you were to name your wound bluntly and concisely. Use one word or the shortest possible phrase to do so, such as the following:

Terminally ill • AIDS • Codependent • Unloved • Disadvantaged • Misfit • Unemployed • Bereaved • Bankrupt • Impotent • Minority • Unstable • Isolated • Disfigured • Molested • Handicapped • Abused • Abandoned • Addicted • Rejected • Adopted • Failure • Depressed • Divorcing • Suicidal

Now picture yourself actually wearing a name tag that announces your wound, your pain, clearly to the whole world so that you can experience in your imagination how it would feel not to try so hard to carry on in spite of what you are going through.

Traditional practices such as wearing black clothing or arm bands after the death of a close relation once served this function, in effect excusing the grieving person during the period of mourning from having to meet society's usual expectations. Today we have largely abandoned such practices, but for the moment wear your "arm band" in the form of your imaginary name tag and excuse yourself from having to appear "normal."

I used to use a variation of this technique when I taught a class called "Understanding Addiction." I would request that all the participants wear a name tag announcing one addiction with which they struggled. Almost everyone learned something from the reactions this exercise elicited. Some felt shame, some felt "found out." Others were only able to name a secondary addiction, not the one that was their primary problem. Many were surprised to feel relief that they no longer had to continue hiding such an important issue. And some simply didn't know which one to choose!

So observe your own reactions as you picture yourself labeled with your wound. Are you ashamed? Too ashamed even in your imagination to state it as bluntly as you might? Do you find another less painful way of putting it, or name a less pressing problem? Or do you feel relieved that now others know because some of them might possibly understand as well? Do you feel wounded in so many ways that it's difficult for you to name only one? There is no right or wrong reaction. Simply observe whatever yours is because it will tell you something about how you are handling your wound.

Admitting to others that our wound exists is a necessary beginning step toward the surrender phase in the formula above. This is why, in twelve-step programs, meetings begin with those present admitting they are alcoholics or drug addicts or overeaters or gamblers or whatever, identifying openly with that which they've tried for so long to hide and which thereby was making their lives unmanageable. Granted, such admissions are more appropriate in an anonymous meeting than in public. Here I'm asking you to admit your wound in your imagination only, because even doing this much helps to free up some of the energy you are using in trying to hide what is at present much of who you are.

We all "wear" our wounds energetically anyway, and we all are able, if only as yet unconsciously, to read each other's energy fields for those wounds. It may truthfully be stated that at a deep level nothing is hidden and there really are no secrets. As we continue to evolve, eventually we will all be able to consciously read one another's energy fields. When that time comes, denial will no longer be possible, and it will be easier to get on with healing ourselves.

Now, on a scale of one to ten, how would you rate your wound's impact on your overall life? Put another way, what percentage of who you are today is your wound? Take a moment to assess this. Many, many people discover that their wound represents 90 percent or more of who they are in terms of their thoughts, feelings, and behavior and how they use their energy on a daily basis. You need to realize that the degree of hold your wound has on you is also the measure of its power to transform you. A profound wound is a theme around which your life will be organized until it is healed and you have received the gift of that wound. Indeed, our wound may be seen as part of a conspiracy between our soul and our life task.

How wounds serve evolution

Sometimes, as in the following case, our wound pushes us toward the path the soul wants us to take but which the personality is resisting. Another way of saying this is that a wound can create the pressure necessary to move us through a healing cycle.

Bankruptcy. Renée's wound was bankruptcy. She was a double Cancer, her sun and ascendant both imbuing her with a craving for security, and she had never recovered from the shock of "losing everything," to use her words. During the years when her former husband's lucrative business began to fail and their marriage was crumbling from the strain of their financial problems, she had sought the help of numerous psychics, desperate for any advice that might put their lives back on track. When she was told several times that yes, their lives were undergoing great changes but this was necessary so that ultimately they each could be happier, her fear only intensified. She couldn't yet know that the coming bankruptcy and divorce would be the catalyst for a more profound healing of a far deeper wound, one that had everything to do with who she was and why she was here.

It was a bright summer day when I first met Renée, but she was dressed all in black. Her long dark hair hung in a straight veil behind which she seemed to be hiding. Her large eyes had a startled look, and a chronic expression of fear and worry lent an almost menacing aspect to her very pretty face. Her aura, like her clothes and her expression, was dark, heavy, and constricted.

Renée had been divorced now for several years, but the loss of all their money bothered her far more than the marriage's ending. Again and again she began her sentences with the words, "When we had money . . ." She had struggled to support herself since the bankruptcy, and her deci-

sion to visit me was triggered by the recent loss of her job
and her inability to find another one, a situation that was
causing her to nearly panic. She had learned from a mutual
friend that I occasionally read horoscopes and once again
she was looking for reassurance. She arrived for her reading
desperate to hear that another job would come along and all
would soon be back to normal. The moment I saw her, my
intuition told me that she wasn't going "back to normal"
ever again, but forward instead into a whole new realm, and
her age helped to confirm my hunch. She was forty-two.

According to the study of astrology, significant changes
can be expected to occur roughly every seven years because
of the aspects Saturn makes to itself in the birth chart. But
at twenty-one, forty-two, sixty-three, and eighty-four Ura-
nus's explosive, revolutionary force is added to Saturn's tendency to instruct us through suffering. Now at the watershed
age of forty-two, I suspected that Renée was due for some
upheaval.

Her chart indicated that there were definitely lessons to
be learned during this lifetime regarding money and material wealth. But more interesting to me were indications of
enormous power and a considerable psychic gift of her own
that would take a most unusual form of expression. When I
told Renée this she immediately looked down at her lap,
shielded by her long curtain of hair. I decided to stop talking and wait. She sat in strained silence for a moment, then
admitted uncomfortably that her grandmother had been a
very gifted psychic. I simply nodded, waiting for the rest of
the story.

Finally she blurted out that all she'd ever wanted to be

was a psychic, that she had the ability to talk with animals, understand their communications with her, and could translate them into words. She also received guidance telling her how to direct energy to help heal sick or injured animals. In fact, she'd had requests from several friends who knew of her abilities for readings of their pets or show stock. Those whose animals suffered from mysterious injuries or illnesses or exhibited puzzling behaviors were especially eager for her help. So far she had refused to read for them, deeply intimidated by the possibility of criticism or worse from any religious groups or individuals who might be threatened by her "powers." When I ventured that she had a wonderful gift that was meant to be used, she shot back, "Obviously you've never been burned at the stake!"

"Have you?" I asked. Her response was to retreat farther behind her veil of hair and wring her hands—beautiful, sensitive hands with long palms and slender tapering fingers. A psychic's hands, a healer's hands.

"All I know is that I want to do this more than anything. I want to help and I know I can, but I'm *so* afraid . . ." Her words trailed off, and she squeezed her hands together so tightly her knuckles turned white.

There was little of help I could say that day, and I didn't see Renée again until two years had passed. She actually had to tell me who she was, shaking my arm and laughing as she tried to jog my memory. I would never have recognized the vibrant, grinning woman with the short cap of shining hair as the same Renée I'd met two years before.

And it had been an incredible couple of years. As every attempt to find a job failed and her financial situation steadily worsened, Renée had very reluctantly begun to do readings of her friends' animals. The results were impressive. Every reading, directed by her Guides, included details about the animal's history she couldn't possibly have known, details that were verified when checked with the present owners or previous owners or breeders. Word of her abilities soon got around when several lame horses were reported by their owners to be sound again after Renée performed her long-distance "energy work" and made recommendations which the owners followed. And she began to develop more confidence as total strangers contacted her for readings on their birds, snakes, horses, cats, and dogs. All she needed was the animal's name and photograph in order to tune in to what the animal was communicating.

Animals for the most part communicate with those human beings who are psychically attuned to them by telepathically "sending pictures" of what they like, what they miss, etc. Renée discovered that sometimes an animal would send a picture of a setting or situation it wanted. This picture often would become a reality soon after, almost as though the animal had been showing Renée its future! For instance, a huge, intimidating guard dog whose owner was trying to find him a new home showed Renée a picture of children riding on his back. Prior to the reading the woman who owned him had never considered him appropriate for a family with children. But a few days after the reading, when a mother of two small tots saw the dog at the park and wanted to take him in spite of his fierce reputation, the woman hesitantly agreed. The next day the new owner called to say her children had been riding the dog all morning and he seemed completely happy.

Proudly, Renée told me that she is now teaching many others how to communicate with animals through her classes and these, along with her readings and healing work, keep her busy and happy. She and her former husband are seeing a lot of each other these days. He has started a new business, one he enjoys greatly, and is finally getting back on his feet financially.

"He understands me and my work better than anyone," she said. "He's always encouraged me to follow this path, but I was too afraid to try until I was on my own and was forced to. Now I wonder how I ever did anything else and so does he."

"And what about money?" I asked.

"Oh, *that*." She laughed. "Actually, I'm doing better financially than I have in years, but I guess it's just not as important to me as it used to be. I was never really that happy during all those years when we had so much money, and yet I was so afraid of losing it." Her voice became reflective. "Maybe because deep down I already knew I was headed toward being on my own and working as a psychic, and I was so afraid to go there again, afraid of what could happen."

I noticed that Renée had used the word *again*, but I didn't make an issue of it. Because she had done so little in this lifetime to develop her psychic perception and healing ability, they were very likely already developed from other incarnations. Bankruptcy was the wound that pushed Renée to reclaim those innate gifts for which she must have paid dearly in another time and place. Only through using them again was she able to lay to rest the "persecuted witch" persona she had subtly carried in her consciousness and even to some degree in her appearance. The healing of that deeper wound from another lifetime healed the one from this lifetime as well. Bankruptcy had served its purpose. It had forced her to surrender to her own healing process. And her fear of persecution caused her to conscientiously examine her motives concerning everything she did in the psychic realm.

"I have to admit," Renée went on, "that I can see in some ways how psychic readings and healing with energy can be interpreted as dangerous and even evil. It's because what you use is *will*, and unless you allow yourself to be guided in all you do by a higher will than your own, it's just selfish self-will that you're using. The only difference between black magic and white magic is whose will is operating—your own selfish will or a higher one that guides you and your work." She paused for a moment.

"I pray all the time now, asking for guidance daily and before every reading I do, every class I teach. I want my only motive to be love. And I can feel that guidance and that love working through me even though things don't always go the way I think they should." She looked at me again, her eyes serious. "I hope I've learned never to misuse my gift, only to use it in the highest way possible."

In this present age when so much glamour is ascribed to psychic gifts such as Renée's, we tend to assume that anyone with such abilities must therefore be very elevated in consciousness. This is no more true than saying that everyone with an innate gift for music or art or higher mathematics is highly evolved spiritually. Every gift that sets us apart—great beauty or talent or intelligence or athletic prowess or whatever—is in fact a test. The greater the gift, the greater the challenge to use it responsibly in spite of the opportunities, the temptations to do otherwise.

I believe Renée was addressing two character defects from previous lifetimes—greed and self-will—which had probably led her to abuse her powers. In this lifetime, her fear of persecution guaranteed that she would use her gifts responsibly or not at all. This was a vital step in her evolution both as a psychic and as a soul incarnate.

Addressing character defects through wounds

As we will see in this chapter, wounds and character defects are closely linked. Sometimes we are wounded because of a defect of character that invites into our life certain kinds of people and events. In other cases our wound may not be a result of a defect of character but is, nevertheless, a means whereby such flaws in us may be addressed and overcome.

Consider now if you will the character defects that your soul may have chosen to address through your own present difficulty or wound. They may well be represented among the so-called seven deadly sins. It has been said that to sin meant originally to be "off the mark." An archer, shooting his arrow and missing the target, had sinned. Such sinning is a necessary and inevitable part of learning to be an archer—and of learning to be a soul in a physical body as well. And just as natural is the inborn urge to overcome missing the mark, to achieve perfection—both as an archer and as a soul incarnate.

Although the seven deadly sins may sound old-fashioned and archaic, they are still very much with us:

Anger

Pride

Gluttony

Avarice

Vanity

Lust

Sloth

These are some of the most natural and predictable human reactions to the pressures and limitations of living in a physical body on the Earth plane. However, as we begin to reconcile with our soul, every such character defect or sin must be refined into its opposite. Anger must evolve into forbearance; pride into humility; gluttony into moderation; avarice into gratitude for what one has; vanity into modesty; lust into intimate partnership; and sloth into willingly carrying one's own weight. To these character defects I would add two more: self-obsession, which must yield to serving others; and self-will, to be replaced by submission to a Higher Will than our own.

Consider for a moment how various wounds provide us with the opportunity to address particular defects of character. If, for instance, we feel unloved, it may be that our self-obsession, our demand for attention, is the real issue. If we are disfigured we may be learning how to base our self-worth on something other than our appearance. If we are economically disadvantaged we may be addressing a long-standing habit of greed. Our lesson then is learning to share what little we have, for sharing is the basis for healthy prosperity.

Each of these examples is greatly oversimplified. In most cases both the expression of our character defects and the conditions that require us to address them are highly personal. So beware, for example, of labeling everyone who is poor as needing to address greed. After all, judging others is another character defect!

Since character defects develop and deepen over many life-times, several incarnations may be required to turn them around into virtues. But with the cultivation of each of these virtues our preoccupation with ourselves is replaced by an attitude that takes into account the welfare of others. Developing this *group con-sciousness* is one of the basic tasks eventually faced by every soul in individual inearnation. We inevitably attract to ourselves the pressures and the opportunities that enable us to do so.

Discovering truth through trauma

Another of our tasks in incarnation is to shed illusion. Often our wounds are linked to some illusion under which we have lived for lifetimes. Even when we are finally able to emerge from such an illusion, it is rare that we can appreciate the magnitude of the process we have undergone. The following story illustrates how the wound of abandonment and the illusion of rescue by a savior may be linked. It shows the complex process by which one indi-vidual worked her way toward Truth.

Jennifer had never given much thought to the subject of past lives, didn't know if she even believed in them, and certainly had never expected to suddenly plunge into experiencing one. Because of an old neck and shoulder injury, she had come to Irene, a highly skilled practitioner of Ida Rolf's deep massage techniques for correcting structural misalignment. This was her ninth of the customary ten Rolfing sessions. Irene was working around Jennifer's mouth and jaw to release habitual tightness there when Jennifer emitted a series of yelps that quickly crescendoed into terrified screams as her body was gripped by violent convulsions.

Because Irene had undergone a similar experience, as had a few of her clients, she immediately recognized what was happening. She grasped Jennifer's hand and calmly but firmly said, "Look at it, tell me what's happening. Tell me what you see." Repeatedly, through Jennifer's screams, Irene insisted that Jennifer describe the ordeal. As Jennifer was able to do so, it began to lose some of its emotional charge and finally she could relate the incident as it unfolded from beginning to end.

"There's a young boy of eight or nine," she reported when she could speak. "He's nothing like I am now and yet I *know* this boy. I know everything he thinks and feels—exactly who he is way down deep inside.

"It's just beginning to get dark outside. We're sitting down to dinner. Everything is so simple, so plain. My father is a farmer."

Struggling to control her emotions, Jennifer continued.

"They kick in the door. We don't even hear them coming. My back is to the door but I see everything on my father's face. It's as though he's saying 'They've come.'

"They're in uniform and they're yelling at my father, but I

don't know what they're saying. Two of them go from room to room breaking our furniture with the butts of their rifles. There is a curtain across the pantry in the kitchen and that's where they find what they're looking for—the radio transmitter my father operated. It's put on the table and smashed in front of us. Then one of the soldiers digs his fingers into my shoulder"—here Jennifer winced sharply, feeling the pain—"and drags me outside. I'm yelling, 'Papa! Papa!'"

Jennifer's tears began again, and her breathing became rapid and shallow as she struggled to continue. "He's herding me around to the back of one of the barns, shoving me hard with his rifle. Then he grabs my shoulders and starts slamming me against the wall, yelling at me. I can't protect myself. My head's banging against the wall and I sort of crumble. Then he kicks me. I'm on the ground and he's kicking and kicking." Jennifer was moaning by now. "I keep thinking 'My father will come and save me. He's so strong. He'll come and stop this.'" She looked up at Irene through streaming tears. "That's all. That's the end."

Irene sat on the table beside Jennifer and held her until once again some of the violent scene's terrifying immediacy had faded. Then she explained what Jennifer already realized—that probably what she was seeing and feeling was the violent end of her most-recent past life. Irene suggested the strong possibility that a theme tied to that cruel death dominated Jennifer's present existence. Could Jennifer possibly identify it?

After a long, still moment Jennifer closed her eyes and replied softly but with conviction, "If I am abandoned I will die." Another long pause and then she added, nodding now,

"That's how I felt as that boy when my father didn't come. Abandoned. And in this lifetime I've been abandoned over and over again."

Irene nodded. "I would guess that abandonment was already an issue for you even before that lifetime because that is how you interpreted the trauma—that you'd been *abandoned*. Instead you might have felt mystified by the assault: 'This isn't *fair*. I've done nothing to deserve this.' In that case you might be dealing with fairness and justice in this present lifetime rather than abandonment. Or you might have felt outrage and a desire for vengeance. Not knowing you had only minutes to live, you might have promised yourself, 'I'll kill him when I grow up.'

"Whatever crystalizes at the moment of a violent death usually sets the pattern for the next lifetime. And the only way that crystallized energy can finally be released is by achieving an entirely different perspective on, in your case, abandonment."

"That's what has happened," Jennifer said. "It's as though I've been in training all my life for what happened last year when my husband died. I loved him—*love* him," she corrected herself, "so much and I was able to let him go, let him leave me, because that's what he chose. I think it's probably both the hardest and the best thing I've ever done."

"Start at the beginning," Irene invited.

Jennifer's story, told with no trace of self-pity, was indeed a saga of abandonment. "My father left my mother when I was four years old. I adored him and suddenly he was gone. I still remember crying and crying, asking where was my daddy? But asking made my mother very angry and dangerous so I learned not to, even though I ached to know. When I was five my mother went away, too, leaving me with my grandmother. Sometimes, maybe once every two or three years, she came for brief visits, but by then she was more like a stranger than a mother. By the time I was about thirteen she stopped coming. My grandmother wouldn't answer any of my questions about either of my parents. She hated my father and was very ashamed of my mother. So again, to keep the peace, I didn't ask.

"My grandmother always let me know how much of a financial burden I was, so when I won a contest at sixteen and started modeling professionally, she was happy I was making money. I was quite successful and at eighteen I met a much older man, a writer. I was flattered by his attention and managed not to notice that he was doing much more drinking than writing. He persuaded me to go to Mexico, where we lived together for about three years in a kind of writers' colony. Then when I was seven months pregnant, he just took off for the States without me.

"I had my daughter, Lori, in Mexico and supported us by managing Americans' vacation homes down there. When it was time for Lori to start school, we came back here to California where I'd grown up.

"I'd had several involvements with different men over the years. Some left me for other women. Some just left me. Most of these men were alcoholics and finally, when I was about thirty-two, I got into Al-Anon. I just couldn't take what life was dealing me anymore. I thought if I went to Al-Anon I'd learn how to hang on to my current alcoholic. He still left but by that time I had learned from the other Al-

Anon members how to handle it better. From what I heard in meetings, I put two and two together and realized that my mother and probably my father, too, had had problems with alcohol. All my life I'd been trying to hang on to one alcoholic or another, terrified they would leave. And in Al-Anon for the first time I began to understand that sometimes the most loving thing you can do is to let someone go. That was the hardest lesson for me. Something in me had always screamed 'Don't leave me, don't leave me! I don't ever want to be left again!'

"After a couple of years in the program I ran into Gregor. If there is such a thing as having a perfect partner, that's what Gregor was for me. We understood each other so perfectly.

"We were married a year later, though I often wonder how he found the courage to make that kind of commitment. My daughter was unwelcoming, to say the least. I had to go to Al-Anon meetings just to be reminded that there were some things I couldn't change, couldn't fix. I wanted so much for us all to be happy together, but it never quite jelled. Gregor was very kind, very patient, very loving. But I almost think Lori missed the drama we'd had with all those alcoholics.

"One night, out of the blue, Lori's father called. He hadn't *ever* laid eyes on her, and here he was on the phone asking her to come visit him in Chicago. After the phone call we talked about the possibility of her going to her father's in the summer. Instead, she ran away. She just got on a bus and went straight to her father's apartment. She was four-teen. Gregor and I did a lot of soul-searching and decided to honor Lori's choice. If we made her come home she could always run away again, and trying to prevent that would have made us all miserable. I think we both believed that she would eventually *want* to come back. But she found an agency in Chicago and started modeling at fifteen, maybe in a way following in my footsteps. Now, at nineteen, she's talking about going into acting. It's a pretty sophisticated lifestyle, but I guess it suits her. Maybe because I didn't get to watch her grow up into the young woman she is today, I still keep waiting for her to come in the back door here, to come home.

"I didn't think anything could be worse than Lori's leaving. Without Gregor and Al-Anon I think I might have actually gone crazy.

"And then two years ago Gregor collapsed from an asthma attack. By the time we reached the hospital, he had no vital signs. They revived him and for days he just cried. Finally he took my hand and told me that he had absolutely no fear and that he was just going to go for it. Those were his exact words: 'I think I'm just going to go for it.'

"I knew what he meant. He was going to *live* instead of trying to stay alive. And I was going to be abandoned again. But I also knew that it was his life, that he had the right to choose. And I knew that his choice was absolutely right.

"Gregor was a woodworker. He loved his work, though the sanding was terrible for his asthma. He loved his friends who lived in the area, most of whom he'd known from boyhood. He loved the mountains where we lived, mountains full of more kinds of chaparral and more kinds of mold from the damp ocean air than almost anywhere on Earth. It was deadly for him, and yet that's where his heart was.

"And so he came home and slowly got his strength back,

and all his friends began coming around. It was almost as though they made pilgrimages to see him. Lori came, too, and told him how much she loved him and how grateful she was for all he'd given her as her stepfather. What happened between them was everything I'd ever hoped for.

"Every moment was so full of life because we *knew* it was all borrowed time. It was as though we were on a honeymoon, so open with each other, so free, so *present*, not taking anything for granted. There were more times than I care to admit when I wanted to grab him and beg him to think of me, to move where he could breathe and be safe and *live*—but we *were* living, the way he wanted to, and that was the only gift I could give him. We had a year before he had another terrible attack, this time alone, in the cab of his truck in the supermarket parking lot."

Jennifer's voice had dropped to a whisper. After a moment she went on speaking. "Sometimes I wonder if I did the right thing. I could have fought with him, insisted he owed it to me to stay alive, tried to make him move away, stop his work. Or I could have never, ever let him out of my sight. But I *know*, even if no one else does, that getting out of his way and letting him have that year of living the way he wanted to was the best thing, the most loving thing I've ever done."

"I know it, too," said Irene, squeezing Jennifer's shoulders, "and I also appreciate what a tremendous initiation you've undergone. An initiation is an expansion of consciousness, a means of opening the mind and heart to a recognition of what already exists in reality. That's what has happened for you.

"I would guess that you've spent lifetimes exploring the themes of loss, abandonment, desertion. You ended your last life certain that abandonment meant death. After losing so many important people in this lifetime, you finally sought help and learned an entirely new approach to your problems. You learned to let go and let God, right? To surrender. And then came the test. You had to allow someone you loved *so* much to make a decision that meant you'd be abandoned again. Do you realize you've demonstrated that the power of love is greater than the power of death? What a victory!"

Jennifer shook her head. "It doesn't *feel* like a victory. Mostly I just miss him so much. . . ."

Irene nodded. "I know. But what if we have an allotted span of years for each lifetime? If that's true, and I believe it is, then look at what happened. Instead of trying to please you, reassure you that he was doing everything he could to postpone the death *you* feared but he didn't, Gregor was able to spend his last year exactly as he chose. And it was *your* victory that made that possible!"

"So victories don't necessarily feel wonderful, do they?" Jennifer asked ruefully.

"Maybe not to the personality. But the soul knows when we've achieved something of the magnitude you have. I think today's experience of your past life was to help you realize what you've accomplished. That may seem like small compensation, but I think finally being able to see how it all fits together is a gift that comes straight from your soul."

"I've been praying to understand why all this had to

happen," Jennifer admitted, "and now, at least to some extent, I do."

Discovering the gift in your wound

Now that you have read examples of how wounds serve us in our spiritual evolution, ask yourself, "How is my wound working on me? In what way is it pressuring me to grow, to expand, to extend my consciousness from the personal to the Universal? How is it helping me to overcome my character defects and free myself from illusion?"

Remember that when Jennifer prayed to be able to understand and *after her wound had served its purpose,* her answers came in a most unusual way. Not all of us will have the kind of graphic past-life experience Jennifer did, along with a person on the spot to explain its significance. In fact, on the subject of past lives it must always be remembered that our present life is our only valid concern. *Everything* with which we need to concern ourselves is contained within it. Pursuing revelations about past lives out of curiosity is at best self-indulgent and at worst unwholesome. We *must* deal with the issues, the pressures, the character defects that are ours in the present. Only when we have overcome our character defects to some degree can our knowing the details of relevant past lives serve any useful purpose. Otherwise they are simply a distraction from or an excuse for our present challenges.

A pertinent spiritual law states that when the time is right, what we are meant to know will be revealed to us without any effort on our part. Jennifer's story demonstrates how this law works in that she did not actively seek her past-life revelations.

The information came to her unsolicited when it could further her understanding and deepen her healing.

It is wise to trust the soul's timing as well as its methods regarding such disclosures. Much that we attribute to chance, to coincidence, is actually the subtle work of the soul. Sometimes our understanding comes from something as simple as overhearing two strangers in conversation. Or we read a book or watch a film and suddenly we *see*, we *know*. Or we dream or meditate and something shifts in us, a realization blossoms that we may never even put into words. But we are changed in some profound and irrevocable way.

Is it all by chance, then? Is there nothing we can do to facilitate what is essentially a divine process?

Like Jennifer, we can ask, we can pray to understand our wound, its purpose, its lesson. We can pray for the strength to not resist its teaching, because whenever we resist addressing our character defects, they don't go away; they worsen. Then yet another healing cycle becomes necessary.

Asking doesn't guarantee that we'll always receive an immediate answer that we can understand, nor does it promise that the pain of the wound will immediately dissipate. But by asking humbly and earnestly, we move toward embracing both the gift of our wound and our own enlightenment.

Five

Why Are My Relationships So Difficult?

Sometimes when we have spent much time and effort seeking answers on a particular subject, the Universe will suddenly provide a relevant clue that illuminates our understanding. For most of my life I have been preoccupied personally and professionally with the nature of human relationships, their dynamics and purpose, and a few years ago I was given one such clue. At the time I was still a practicing psychotherapist but was feeling a growing frustration with the approach to understanding human behavior that I'd been trained to take. One day I was talking with a professional psychic about the difficulties we each encountered in our work.

"What annoys me the most," my friend stated heatedly, "is when my clients use what they believe to be a situation from a past life to justify some perfectly idiotic thing they're doing in the present!" She then described a case in point, a woman she had seen a few weeks before, whose marriage, my friend quickly intuited, was a hopeless misalliance. In view of the obvious agony for both parties, she boldly stated her case. "You two should have split up years ago," she told the client bluntly. But the woman merely smiled enigmatically, explaining that early in her marriage she'd consulted another psychic. From him she had learned that in another lifetime, her husband had been her son, whom she'd deserted and who, as a result, had suffered terribly and died.

"So you see," said the woman, her voice bright with determination, "I couldn't *possibly* leave him again in this lifetime."

"Well, you'd better," my psychic friend informed her, "because as it is, you're killing him all over again!"

Relationships and destiny

For years I was haunted by the story of that woman's determination to secure her husband's safety and comfort at any cost, all the while achieving precisely the end she had hoped to avoid. It seemed to me a cryptic allegory, a relationship version of the classic novel by John O'Hara *Appointment in Samarra*. Perhaps you remember that tale, in which a man learns in the marketplace one morning that Death will come to fetch him that very night. Desperate to avoid his fate, the terrified man flees, traveling all day and late into the evening until he is sure he has put enough distance between himself and Death that he can safely stop and rest. There, late at night in faraway Samarra, he suddenly finds himself face-to-face with Death, who compliments him for being able to keep their appointment, all the more surprising since it was made for a place so far from his home.

This chilling tale and the story of the psychic's client both appear to be saying the same thing: that we may actually seal our fate through the very efforts we make to avoid it. Indeed, it would seem that just when we think we are escaping, we are, if we but knew it, running as fast as we can to embrace precisely what we dread. Particularly in relationships, there seem to exist hidden undercurrents that use our conscious desires and intentions to produce the effect opposite of what we intend. Indeed, it would seem that any significant relationship actually has an independent life of its own with a purpose quite hidden from our conscious awareness.

Doesn't this fit to some degree with your own experience? Haven't you ever felt, as I have, that contrary to all your conscious wishes and motives regarding someone close to you, there was an invisible and irresistible force that drove your relationship and defined it? That, like the psychic's client, your own best efforts to sail away from disaster toward a safe harbor simply served instead to drive you aground on the very shoals you were trying so hard to avoid? But if this is the case, why is it so? What purpose is being served?

The true purpose of relationships

When I look back from the perspective of nearly fifty years of living, I realize that I've always been trying to find the basic *key* that would explain why we human beings often endure such suffering through involvement with our fellows. In my fifteen years as a psychotherapist, I discovered a great deal—but not the *key*. Like someone unable to see the forest for the trees, I was standing too near, was too enmeshed in the details of my own and my clients' lives to see the overall picture. I needed greater distance. So Life gave me what I needed. The decks were cleared and for seven years I watched, I read, I pondered—and gradually I began to understand.

What I finally realized is that our most significant relationships exist for a very different reason than we believe, either personally as individuals or collectively as a society. Their true purpose is *not* to make us happy, *not* to meet our needs, *not* to define for us our niche in society, *not* to keep us safe . . . *but to cause us to grow toward the Light*.

The simple fact is that together with those people with whom we are bonded through blood or marriage or deep kinship, we have set upon a charted course with hazards and hindrances designed to carry us from one point of evolution to another. In fact, we would do well when seeking to understand the often troubled nature of our human relationships if we reminded ourselves that there is an impeccable, implacable efficiency in the Universe, the goal of which is the evolution of consciousness. And always, *always* the fuel for that evolution is desire.

At the very root of Creation itself is the desire of Life to manifest in form. This is the will-to-be. And implicit in every form, from the lowliest to the most evolved, is the desire or the will-to-become. To become what? A greater, fuller, more complete, pure, and perfect expression in physical matter of the Force behind Creation. This will-to-become exists in every province, from the tiniest atom to the sum of the physical Universe and from the most exalted regions of existence on down to this dense physical plane in which we, humanity, dwell. Although our necessarily limited perspective would sometimes seem to deny the fact, we human beings are driven right along with all the rest of Creation toward that Becoming.

The soul, which sends us along the Path, is compelled by the desire to become closer to God. We, as personalities, facilitate this goal by our own natural desire to pursue pleasure and avoid pain. For those of us whose fundamental needs for food, shelter, and safety are met relatively easily, it is primarily our human relationships that provide both the carrot and the stick to keep us moving forward. Thus the difficult child; the rebellious teenager; the disapproving parent or the cold, rejecting one or the needy, smothering one; the friend who betrays us; the boss who exploits us; the object of our love who doesn't love us in return; the spouse who disappoints us or criticizes us, who leaves us or dies; those persons who occupy our thoughts and play upon our emotions, with whom we live, for whom we yearn, about whom we worry, against whom we complete or rebel, for whose sake we sacrifice and suffer—all of them push and pull and prod us along the Path we share with them, the Path toward Awakening.

Awakening from what? From the illusions we still harbor about ourselves, about the world, and about our place within that world; from the character defects that we have yet to admit and overcome. And, as we advance to a higher spiral on the Path, relationships help us awaken gradually from every one of our selfish desires.

The following story describes how one such Awakening was brought about as a result of a stressful parent-child relationship.

Marleen, at twenty-two, married a man whose last name was followed by the roman numeral IV. Obviously his was a family that took its heritage and heirship seriously. Every one of Marleen's four pregnancies in six years ended in spontaneous abortion, and after the fourth miscarriage, which was accompanied by serious medical complications, she was told she would never again be able to conceive. This sad news struck a deathblow to the marriage. Her husband divorced her and quickly married again, this time to a woman who promptly obliged him by producing a tiny number V.

Marleen, crushed by the double loss of her marriage and her hope for a family, finally pulled herself together and returned to school for her master's degree in journalism. After graduation, determined to reconcile herself as happily as possible to a childless future, she energetically pursued a career of writing and travel.

When she was in her midthirties Marleen accepted a marriage proposal from a man who had been a longtime friend and who had gradually come to mean much more to her. Expecting with this second marriage to experience little change in her lifestyle, she was amazed after a year had gone by to find that she was pregnant. In due time a bright-eyed and beautiful but fussy infant was born.

Little Caitlin was a demanding baby who grew into an imperious child. Her mother, so grateful for her existence, found it difficult to say no or set limits or frustrate in any way her precious daughter, whom she had taken to calling her "miracle child." Caitlin's father, a quiet, easygoing man, liked setting limits no better than his wife, and soon Caitlin was an unbridled despot at home and an ill-mannered terror in public. Marleen and her husband tacitly agreed on their interpretation of their daughter's behavior. No, this was not a tyrannical and uncontrollable child but a bold, fearless, and irrepressibly individualistic one. They didn't notice that several of their friends had begun to avoid the three of them.

After some years at home with Caitlin, years that were far more of a trial than Marleen would admit to herself, she resumed her writing career. Working as a stringer for the local newspaper, she was eventually assigned to report on several controversial environmental issues about which she held strong personal convictions. Never one to deliberately court controversy, she searched for ways to avoid head-on collisions with her editor and readers while remaining true to herself. The pressure began to build.

At home things were heating up as well. Caitlin was escalating her dictatorial demands daily while Marleen continued to tell everyone how lucky, how blessed she and her husband were to have this special child. But in a separate compartment of her mind Marleen began entertaining fantasies of stepping back into her single life of independence and world travel.

Suddenly, the way we often do when we've backed ourselves into a corner, Marleen found herself taking an inexplicably fierce and furious stand. One day, angry over a relatively trifling matter, she threatened to leave her husband *and* her daughter. Hearing herself voice this threat was as much a shock to Marleen as it was to her husband. Seven-year-old Caitlin responded by shouting her mother down with counterthreats of her own. Numbly, Marleen drew her husband into their bedroom.

While a screaming Caitlin kicked and pounded at their locked door, her mother and father finally began to face the nightmare their lives had become. The very thought of having to manage his headstrong daughter alone was so appalling to Marleen's mild-natured husband that he quickly agreed with his wife that limits were needed. Together they worked out a plan to try curbing their daughter's willfulness.

Encouraged by the support of their remaining long-suffering friends, who noticed their efforts and strongly approved, Caitlin's parents stopped yielding to her demands, stopped buying her off or placating her. While she threw tantrums in public and at home, hurled imprecations and threatened them with undying hatred, they set reasonable limits and calmly enforced them. They disciplined her, encouraged and comforted each other, and found to their surprise that their affection for each other grew and their sex life improved. Both felt more energetic and more excited about life than they had in years. Even at its worst, their present battle of wills with Caitlin cost them less energy than had all their years of trying to keep the peace by tiptoeing around her.

Eventually, their struggle was over. A gracious and far more secure child emerged in place of one who had felt overwhelmed by the burden of a freedom and a power she had been far too immature to handle.

Marleen, too, emerged from this difficult passage a more balanced person. At a subtle level she had, since Caitlin's birth, let the little girl do all the speaking up, all the fighting and demanding while she remained passive and beatifically smiling. Now a fresh sense of her own very considerable strength inspired her to propose a column to her editor, one in which she addressed a variety of subjects including the issues that divided the community, from her own personal perspective. Her editor agreed, guessing that her naturally gentle humor would entertain even those who opposed her views. Today this woman who once had such difficulty taking a stand with her daughter now lets her opinions be known at home as well as in print.

It is important to understand that this is not simply a story of how two parents finally learned the wisdom of setting limits and the necessity of discipline in child rearing. The fact that the family situation got so out of hand before it was even acknowledged, much less confronted, indicates that one or more important defects of character were manifesting in the parents and needed to be overcome in order for the obvious problem to be resolved. Indeed the discipline problem arose *because* of the existence of these character defects and then grew in severity, demanding that these flaws be addressed. For many long and trying years, Marleen, with the unconscious complicity of her husband, denied both the reality of her child's behavior and, more important, her own emotional reactions to it. She did all this so that she could live out her mythical role of perfect parent to a special child of destiny.

Creating and dispelling illusion

Such a myth, one which has the power to profoundly affect our lives and our judgment, is esoterically referred to as a "glamour." We ourselves create these glamours, these illusions under which we labor until their spell is broken. Eventually every glamour which enthralls us produces precisely the tests necessary in order to break our illusion and dissipate the glamour.

In Marleen's case the very pressures generated by her attempt to live out her mother-and-child fantasy finally rendered her willing to relinquish it. Obviously hers was a far more subtle test than whether she would kill or steal from or deliberately harm another person for her own selfish purposes. Her honesty and integrity when dealing with others was well developed. Marleen had evolved to the point where she had to confront a far more subtle issue: her capacity for *personal* dishonesty; that is, her capacity to delude herself with a cherished vision of who she wanted herself and her daughter to be.

Because glamours are always based on the selfish desires of the personality, they are always unwholesome. They exist on the astral plane, where they have their own characteristic substance, shape, sound, and even odor. They can be seen psychically as a kind of glittering miasma, a thick, shiny fog full of pictures, scenes, events, and often images of other people. They can feel sticky like glue or snag like Velcro. Their odor is repellent even if sweet, a cloying or slightly decayed smell. Their sound is an unpleasant buzzing, clattering, or roaring. Glamours have a life of their own that resists destruction, and they are always opposed to our enlightenment.

Weaning ourselves from our cherished fantasies with which we identify so thoroughly requires an objectivity we simply don't possess while in their thrall. Usually a crisis is necessary before we can be weaned from these creations of ours that hold us captive.

The process of awakening

Having read Marleen's story, you might find yourself wondering what glamours cloud your own thoughts, perceptions, and actions. You might wish you could name them and confront them and put them to rest. Indeed, you may feel that you have been trying for a long time to see yourself more clearly.

In today's sophisticated psychological climate many of us consciously strive to achieve greater inner awareness. Ours may be a sincere desire for spiritual development or we may be fueled by emotional pain. Often it is a combination of both these factors that impels us to read books, attend lectures, buy self-improvement tapes, join a support group, seek a religion we can believe in, a teacher we can follow, a therapist we can trust. But no matter how dedicated we are to our awakening, we nevertheless unconsciously fear and therefore resist the very process we are courting. This fundamental ambivalence arises because we intuitively know that to awaken to any degree means that we, like Marleen, must relinquish the fantasies with which we identify so deeply.

An apt metaphor for the awakening process in any of us is the biblical story of Saul, who obsessively persecuted the earliest Christians. When, on the way to Damascus, he was struck blind and helpless, he was confronted with his deeper spiritual blindness and awakened to the fact of his self-righteousness. Through this awakening he was converted to the very beliefs he had so violently opposed. As was the case with Saul and Marleen and the woman described at the beginning of this chapter, who clung to her fantasy of protecting the husband she made miserable, our every awakening demands that we acknowledge and surrender to *precisely that which we've spent our lifetime(s) most energetically resisting and denying.*

No wonder we're scared.

And no wonder something as unavoidable and as compelling as our human relationships is often required to keep us in the game and playing for all we're worth with those perilous fires of Awakening.

Desire in the service of evolution

Remember, desire is the key to all evolution throughout all of Creation. Within the human realm it is our own personal desires that have the power to seduce us into deeper (and sometimes more desperate) involvements with other people. We want to be seen as a certain kind of person or we want love or approval, admiration, respect, comfort, sex, material goods, security, companionship, status, power, help of some kind or relief or protection. To the same degree that we are seduced by our desire, we may be inducted, eventually, into greater awareness. A formula for all such awakenings fueled by desire might well be written as simply as this:

seduction (by desire) → induction (into awareness)

The world *seduction* conjures up, for most of us, an image of someone so irresistibly appealing that we yield to this person in spite of our better judgment. The fact is, we cannot be seduced except through our own desires. Those persons with the greatest capacity to facilitate our further unfoldment are the ones who generate in us the strongest feelings and toward whom we find ourselves inexorably drawn. Though we think of seduction primarily as a sexual event, we are actually constantly seduced by our own glamours, reflecting as they do our character defects.

For instance, it is often the case that we choose someone for certain qualities we are unwilling to develop or express ourselves. We claim to admire these qualities or abilities in this other person, yet feel betrayed when we ourselves are forced to develop those same qualities. Daphne, whose story follows, was seduced by her husband's apparent capabilities as a caretaker, while he was attracted to what he perceived as her feminine frailty. As their fortunes changed, both partners were inducted into the other's role and condition.

Until her widowed mother remarried at fifty-two, Daphne lived at home, comfortably secure in the familiar surroundings she'd known since childhood. She'd tried living on her own a few times, but one or another of her frequent and mysterious ailments had necessitated her return, sooner or later, to her mother's home and solicitude. When her new stepfather presented his bride with a lovely condominium that bordered the golf course where they'd met, Daphne was forced to take the hint. Even as she moved out, she was looking around seriously for the next person who would take care of her.

Hamilton seemed the most likely candidate. His judicious purchases of commercial real estate had made him, in the course of a few years and in spite of the financial setback of a divorce five years earlier, a wealthy man. With broad shoulders and towering stature, he gave every appearance of strength in spite of the fact that a bout with rheumatic heart disease in childhood still forced him to curtail his physical activities. Next to his massive physique, Daphne, with her slight build, pale skin, and huge eyes seemed even more fragile.

They had met at a conference on alternative medical treatments and had dated regularly ever since, with Hamilton occasionally hinting cautiously of marriage. He hadn't seemed to mind Daphne's constant references to her delicate health or her obvious reluctance to establish an existence independent of her mother. His former wife had been aggressively self-sufficient, and he found Daphne's pliant dependence a refreshing contrast.

When Daphne and Hamilton married within a few short months of her leaving home, it was with the understanding that her health was too delicate for the rigors of pregnancy, childbirth, and parenthood. The first flashing forth of Daphne's very considerable will occurred when Hamilton suggested that eventually her health might improve enough to make having children a possibility. She attacked with cold fury. Didn't he understand? It was absolutely out of the question!

That will became more frequently evident as they made their home together in the house Ham had inherited from his parents. Daphne rapidly instituted massive and costly renovations that when completed effectively divided the house into two separate units. Citing her poor health and consequent need for quiet, Daphne staked her claim to one side while relegating her husband to the other. And Ham, embarrassed in the light of his wife's frailty by the implied selfishness of his objections, quietly acquiesced.

They had been married several years when the economy began to decline sharply and one by one the leased spaces in Ham's commercial buildings were vacated. Soon the remaining rents weren't sufficient to cover the mortgage payments on many of the properties. Straining to save his holdings while property values continued to plummet, Ham came down with a flu virus and never recovered his strength. After several months, his doctor ascertained that this particular virus had further weakened his already damaged heart muscle. Now it was difficult for him to get enough oxygen to function normally either physically or mentally. Every effort left him weak and exhausted.

Daphne, citing the double strain of their troubled finances and Ham's semi-invalidism, collapsed. For a few weeks she languished in bed, competing with her husband for the role of patient needing nursing. But this time no one appeared to coddle her. And since indulging her hypochondria clearly meant losing all hope of future security, Daphne began to rally. Her driving need to feel secure and protected made her an apt pupil as she educated herself regarding the state of Ham's holdings.

After careful study and using what help Ham could give her, Daphne began to make careful decisions about which properties to keep and which to sacrifice in a plummeting market. She offered more attractive rents to the remaining tenants in an effort to ensure that they stayed on, and gradually took a far more personal interest and active hand in the management of each property than Ham ever had. Along the way she took classes and passed one examination after another, finally ending up with her real estate broker's license.

Today Ham's health remains much the same. He has difficulty concentrating or exerting himself for any length of time. His condition has made him quite passive and very dependent. Daphne, whose studied fragility was always undergirded by a strong practical sense, long ago rented out her half of their home and moved back in with Ham. She applies the rent to paying a part-time housekeeper/nurse who takes care of Ham and the house while Daphne attends to business elsewhere.

Daphne's reputation as a manager of commercial property is growing. Her own offices now occupy an entire floor of Ham's most upscale office building, and she has become a moderately successful businesswoman in spite of the slack real estate market. She still complains far too much about her delicate health, but she rarely has time now to address her various vague medical problems. Her relationship with Ham is rather empty, but then it always was. Sex and intimacy were never that important to either of them, and divorce is out of the question. She could never leave someone so ill. With poor health herself, she knows what a terrible blow that would be—and besides, all those properties that he brought to their marriage are still in his name. . . .

The marriage between Daphne and Ham was largely motivated by selfish desires on both their parts. Ham liked the idea of being strong and in control, while Daphne wanted to remain weak and be protected. Both were willing to make considerable sacrifices in order to play their chosen roles: Daphne submitting to life as the wife of a man she didn't really love; Ham foregoing sex or even much companionship from his partner.

To attribute the reversal of their roles simply to a twist of Fate would deny the fact that these two people deliberately chose each other in order to enhance their cherished images of themselves. It was this as much as their financial difficulties and Ham's failed health that set each of them up for the next stage of their personal unfoldment.

Obviously there is still a strong motive of selfishness fueling Daphne's present actions. That will likely be true for many lifetimes to come. But she is learning to be more overt rather than covert in the expression of her personal strength, and that is a definite advance for her. Ham's semi-invalidism is acquainting him personally with that very condition he found so appealing when he perceived it in Daphne. Through his condition he's learning and understanding some hard lessons about the true nature of strength and weakness, personal power and its loss through poor health versus its willful abdication. Daphne and Ham are learning some of the lessons with which Life confronts us in the context of our relationships.

If, as in the above case, some relationships can force us into becoming what we've tried to avoid, other relationships can teach us how to avoid becoming what we don't want to be. Many of us take lessons in what *not* to be from our parents.

The choice of a difficult parent

At the time of each incarnation we choose, under the direction of our soul, those parents who will not only provide us with the appropriate physical vehicle for the coming lifetime but who will help further our spiritual development. Desiring evolution, our

soul assigns us to our parents not because they will give us everything our personality may wish for but because they provide
some important part of what we require in order to advance along
the Path. Any of us who feel we might have gotten farther along
in life if only we'd had parents who loved us more, encouraged
us more, understood us better would do well to remember that
these are the desires of the personality, not the needs of the soul.
Whatever we might or might not accomplish in the outer world
is of small consequence in relation to the progress we achieve
in a given lifetime on behalf of our soul. Because of our reactions
to them, difficult parents can often contribute greatly to that
progress.

An example of this contribution is described in the following
story:

Judge George K. had been in court one way or another all
his professional life. After long years spent prosecuting the
various kinds of crimes that were committed in the county
in which he lived, he was elected to the Superior Court, a
position he filled with the same zeal he'd brought to his
other occupations.

In appearance the judge resembled nothing so much as a
tonsured monk who had exchanged his order's robe for
that of the courtroom. Round, balding, apple cheeked, with
a droll smile often playing at the corners of his mouth,
everything about him seemed to belie his stern and sober
career—unless you happened to notice the deep vertical
crease between his brows and the penetrating glitter of
his bright brown eyes. In that case you would find yourself

trying to reconcile your impression of his jolly amiability with these hints that he had a harder and far more calculating side.

Judge K. had been married three times. Each wife had left him for reasons neither George nor the wives understood. Sooner or later each of these women had reasons to be separated from him temporarily and then found that she did not want to return home. Each then took steps to make the separation permanent, giving vague reasons for doing so. His first wife, taking on their two burgeoning adolescents single-handedly, explained lamely, "It must be time for me to be on my own." The second wife, thirty-eight when she filed for divorce, claimed, "Maybe it's my version of an early midlife crisis." The third simply stated, "I never knew how important my career was to me." These marriages and divorces occurred over a twenty-five-year period and the ex-wives, once free of him, often continued to describe George as a "wonderful man" but rarely had anything to do with him again if they could help it. His acquaintances, observing his marital history, thought that for such a "wonderful" man he certainly had bad luck with women.

The two children, a boy and girl, kept in close contact with their mother after leaving home but connected with their father only when they had to: a card and a call on Father's Day, a request that George play his appropriate role at their respective weddings, occasional brief visits at Christmas or when a new baby was born. They, too, seemed to avoid him, though he had been punctilious about support payments to their mother and rigorously exercised his visitation rights after the divorce.

George rarely drank and never smoked and, despite his love of good food, there was something of the puritan about him.

Although he was reasonably well liked in the courts, no defense attorney would willingly try a case before Judge K. if it could be helped. George was known by prosecutors and defense attorneys alike as tough; the sentences he handed down, though always technically justifiable according to the letter of the law, were frequently severe and even extreme.

"He's such a nice guy everywhere but on the bench" went the small talk.

Now George was back in the town where he had been born, a town he hadn't visited since his family moved away thirty years before. The funeral of his closest childhood friend, Billy, had brought him back. His friend's Aunt Hattie, an eccentric old woman and the last of Billy's family still living, had insisted that George visit her before flying home. George had never met her before, though he vaguely remembered Billy talking about his mother's sister Hattie, who lived abroad and was an actress.

Sitting in the well-remembered living room of Billy's family home where Hattie now lived alone, George was struggling to keep his usual air of genial dignity intact. But something in Hattie's penetrating gaze was causing his well-polished demeanor to dissolve. This difficult old woman wouldn't help his efforts at small talk along with her share of anecdotes or even by listening to his.

Hattie had served him cake. Now as she poured coffee she asked innocently, "Did Billy ever tell you I read palms?" George's mouth was full of cake, but his eyes widened with

alarm as he shook his head. She seated herself and confi-
dently reached for his hands, laughing with an old woman's
rusty chuckle.

"It's true. I've always been the eccentric one. But it's important in the theater to know which people you can trust
and those you need to watch carefully. Besides," she added
playfully, "it's fun and I'm nosy. Every actor has to be a psy-
chologist, you know. If we're any good at all, we must know
what makes people tick. Palmistry was the easiest way for
me to study types. And I could make a living with readings
when parts were few and far between."

She stopped chatting for a moment. Silently she drew her
fingers along each one of his, flexed his hands backward,
squeezed his palms in various places. Tense and uncomfortable, George told himself it wouldn't hurt to indulge this
eccentric old woman for another half hour and then he
could escape. When she looked up again she spoke quietly.

"I want to tell you something that may be very difficult
for you to hear. Your hands say that there is, in your nature,
a great deal of cruelty." George launched into an immediate, spluttering protest, but she stopped him with a gentle
smile. "Oh, I know. I'm sure all your friends, even Billy if he
were here, would tell me you are the finest of men. Even
your hands tell me you're trying to be." She looked into his
eyes with obvious sympathy. "But it's hard work, isn't it?"
His face was growing red with anger. How much did he
have to put up with just to be polite?

Hattie continued. "Tell me about your parents. What
were they like?"

Relieved that the conversation had veered away from *him*,

he answered, "My mother is a wonderful woman. And I don't mind telling you, I was her favorite. She tried to make up for the way my father treated me.

"Now, if you want to talk about cruelty, my *father* was *cruel*. Not physically. Oh, no. He was more subtle than that. It was his idea to name me after my mother's brother who was a complete failure, a dullard, totally lacking any ambition. Then, the whole time I was growing up, he compared me to Uncle George, implying that I was just like him. And no matter what I did to prove my intelligence, no matter what I accomplished, he always saw me as barely one step away from being good-for-nothing."

He'd just begun to warm to his subject when she shunted him off course, asking, "Will you tell me the date of your birthday?" He brusquely muttered the information as Hattie reached for her ephemeris from the nearby bookshelf.

"This book contains the position of the planets for every day of the century," she explained while looking up the date he had given her.

"I thought so," she said with satisfaction, tapping the page and showing him columns of tiny numbers. "Mars was in Taurus when you were born. Hitler had that, too, you know. It can indicate a cruel streak just as the combination of some of the features in your hand does: your prominent lower mount of Mars, your club thumbs, the overall thickness of your hands and the bluntness of your fingers. And yet there are indications of a fine mind and considerable sensitivity, too. Sometimes people come into a lifetime with several indications of a penchant for brutality. But they have already achieved sufficient consciousness to realize this propensity must be overcome. That means they have quite a task in front of them because they spend their lifetime at war with their own nature." George was incensed by her words but Hattie, oblivious, was smiling at him.

"You know what I think? I think you deliberately chose that father of yours in order to create in yourself an aversion to cruelty. I bet you've spent your whole life trying not to be like your father."

"That's right, I have!" George nearly shouted, annoyed that she was right about a decision he'd made so early he couldn't ever remember not being committed to it.

"And I like to think I've succeeded. I'm exactly his opposite. He belittled me, my sisters and brothers, my mother, all our relatives, everyone. No one was good enough or smart enough to suit him."

"And you don't do any of those things."

"No, I don't! I've always been extremely careful to be encouraging to my children and to each of my wives."

"Has anyone ever accused you of lacking spontaneity?" Hattie asked. George felt sidetracked somehow. This crazy old woman kept changing the subject.

"Actually, my kids used to say that I should loosen up . . . and a constant complaint from every one of my wives was that I wasn't what they called 'fun.' But I never understood that. I decided very early that I was always going to be cheerful. I never grumbled like my father did." Suddenly he stopped, shaking his head dully. "Sometimes I wonder why I've tried so hard. People who don't really know me like me well enough, but people who are close to me—well, there aren't any people close to me. I've never understood it." Hattie patted his hand.

"I'm going to help you to understand," she said. "Imagine that there is a school where you can go to learn to be kind. You weren't born knowing how, but you were determined that, even though you'd have to study hard and practice constantly, you were going to learn. And imagine that before you ever got to the school, you were anything but kind. Like your father, you were cruel and hurtful to others for no reason other than long-standing habit.

"Right now you're in maybe second grade of this School of Kindness. You have a long way to go before what you're learning comes so naturally to you that you don't have to make an effort or even think about it. You're still working on inhibiting the cruel impulse, the unkind word, the criticism, the insult, even the brutal act. But since you've entered this school you've been afraid that if you don't hide those aggressive, hurtful tendencies from others, you won't even be allowed to stay and learn. So you work very hard to cover up what is still a basic part of you, a part you've become ashamed of and are afraid to acknowledge even to yourself."

The man of law who sat before her, who as a young attorney had nearly made an art form of the skillful argument, found himself too dazed to debate what this silly woman was saying.

"The hardest part," Hattie continued, "is that the impulses that are still a natural part of you build up pressure to be released. You've been able to release a lot through your work."

George nodded, his eyes on the floor. "When I was a prosecutor my second wife asked me how I could handle my job emotionally. She couldn't stand hearing about the violence and brutality I had to deal with every day." He looked up at Hattie. "But I loved my work."

"Of course you did. When you were fighting against the cruelty people did to one another, you were fighting against it in yourself, too. That's what you came here to overcome. But"—here she softly squeezed both his hands with hers— "you become dangerous when you cannot acknowledge your own cruelty. You then externalize your own dark side and try to stamp it out, crush it in others—those whom you once prosecuted and who now appear before you in court."

"I'm nothing like them!" The judge's voice contained both menace and desperation. "I would never commit a crime!"

"Do you remember the story by Somerset Maugham called 'Rain'?" Hattie seemed to be veering off the subject again. "It was made into a movie called *Sadie Thompson*. In it a puritanical preacher takes it upon himself to save a happy-go-lucky, hedonistic young woman from a life of prostitution. He has just about convinced her to change her wicked ways when a violent tropical rainstorm traps them alone together in a hut. All his long-denied feelings and urges overtake him and he rapes her." She paused for a while, letting the story do its work, then continued. "We become dangerous when we deny any part of our humanity, even a part of which we're ashamed."

It was quiet between them for a long moment. Then George asked in a low voice that mixed resentment and defeat, "Why did every one of my three wives leave me? Why do my children avoid me? No matter what you say, I never hurt any of them!"

"I can't be sure, but I think it's because first of all, they don't really trust you. They sense, perhaps subconsciously, the constant effort you're making to suppress an aspect of your nature, and they find it hard to be with you. And second, I would guess that the cruelty that is in you leaks out in some ways so subtle that none of you are able to identify it, but it does its damage nevertheless."

"Then it's hopeless!" George nearly bellowed. "I can't win, no matter how hard I try."

"It's nothing of the sort. You've already spent decades learning not to be overtly hurtful, *really* learning it. Granted, it's been a bit like driving your car with the brakes on. But if, before, every time you drove your car it went a hundred miles an hour and killed someone, then it's a great improvement to learn how to drive it with the brakes on. The problem is that your pride forces you to deny the angry, aggressive part of you that *likes* to go a hundred miles an hour and damn the consequences. You might try acknowledging that part and resisting it *consciously*.

"You should be very proud of yourself actually. For one lifetime you've already gotten quite a lot accomplished."

George sat back in his chair and stared hard at this strange old lady who was saying these extraordinary things to him about his life. He pulled himself together and said coldly, "I don't want to seem ungrateful for all the time you've taken, but I don't believe *any* of this. Reading palms! That's really far-fetched, you know."

Standing up and guiding him to the door, Hattie patted his arm, smiling so broadly her sharp blue eyes nearly disappeared in the folds of her crinkled skin. "I don't know if I believe any of it either. But it does seem to make *some* sense, doesn't it? Why not let a bit of time go by and see if our little talk is of any use to you? What can be the harm in that?"

And on that rather inconclusive note, George and Hattie bid one another good-bye.

George had been given an unusual opportunity, albeit one he might fail to regard as a blessing, to know himself better. His experience with Hattie's palm reading was rather like that of an alcoholic who, perhaps because of a drunk-driving offense, is forced by the court to attend Alcoholics Anonymous meetings. The drinker may refuse to admit a problem exists, may continue to drink, but will never again be able to achieve quite the same degree of nonchalance about his relationship with alcohol. The phrase in AA is "Come on in and we'll ruin your drinking for you."

This is what happened to George. His tightly maintained view of himself as a genuinely nice person had been punctured, even if only for a few private moments, by a dubious stranger. But from that hour on he would find it more difficult to convince himself and others that his character contained only goodwill. As in the case of the alcoholic, George had only two choices. With the encouragement he'd received from Hattie, he might now admit that though he might wish otherwise, there was a sadistic element in his makeup. Then he could employ the energy previously used to maintain his facade and his denial to now *consciously* monitor any such impulses. Such efforts at achieving rigorous personal honesty in this sensitive area of his life would make him a far more relaxed and genuine person. Or he could continue to deny the existence of this cruel element in his nature—but from now on, because of what happened with Hattie, the effort required to do so would be far greater.

George's meeting with Hattie was a healing cycle. Healing cycles don't necessarily mean that we heal. They are merely opportunities for healing. We have a choice as to how we respond when they occur. But every time we refuse or ignore an opportunity to heal, we are guaranteeing that the next cycle will be more pressing, more disruptive, more difficult to deny.

Practice in redefining relationships

What did George do with his invitation to encounter himself at a deeper, truer level? In all likelihood he tried his best to ignore the invitation, discredit the person who had offered it, and go on as before with his life. This is the response most of us have, most of the time, to our healing cycles. After all, if it were easy to admit to consciousness the parts of ourselves we fear and despise, we'd all do it a lot sooner and in response to far less pressure than is usually required.

If you believe you would welcome the chance to better understand your own nature, ask yourself the following questions. Because hearing your own voice will make them much more powerful and real, ask yourself aloud, "What about me? Has life invited me to be more honest about my own dark side? And how have I responded to such invitations—with frankness or with fear? What would be the worst thing I could find out about my own nature? Can I accept that this may very well dwell buried within me, fueling both my horror of it and my revulsion and judgmental attitude toward those who cannot hide this aspect of themselves? Have I known people who have helped create an aversion in me for these traits? Can I acknowledge that perhaps I should feel grateful to them for the part they've played in my own evolution?

Obviously, these aren't questions for which there are "correct" answers listed somewhere in this book to be looked up after you've pondered them. These are the questions all of us who would consciously participate in our own evolution must ask ourselves again and again and again. They are samples of the way each of us needs to begin to examine all that goes on within us and around us in life. When we learn to habitually ask these kinds of questions and seek these kinds of answers, we will find that a new paradigm or worldview emerges—one that utterly alters everything. Through that new vision it is possible to comprehend the integrated nature of relationships, events, and evolution. Through it we can *know* that we live in a Cosmos, not a Chaos. We can begin to appreciate the way each person, each life fits as a meaningful part of a greater Order in which all of us, individually and in concert together, play a vital and magnificent part.

Six

How Did I End Up with These Relatives?

Two years ago while shopping I bumped into a woman friend I hadn't seen for a while. From the time of our first meeting twenty years before, she has been one of my favorite people, effervescently bubbling with humor and enthusiasm, a happy partner to her husband. Together they have what to my mind is a nearly perfect marriage. Their shared passion for the natural sciences has led them and their children around the world on fascinating vacations spent swimming with sea turtles, counting nesting puffins, playing with porpoises, and observing iguanas.

Sitting down over coffee expecting to hear about the latest exotic travels and her children's most recent achievements, I was surprised to see her face cloud over when I asked what they as a family had been up to lately. I listened as my friend told about the hellish year she and her husband had just been through with their sixteen-year-old son. This previously cheerful, cooperative child and model student had become virtually impossible to live with. There had been problems at school and numerous scrapes with the police as well as daily volcanic eruptions at home. Now my friend and her husband were having serious arguments for the first time in their married life. The whole family was seeing a counselor who suggested the possibility of a temporary foster home for the boy.

"You ask yourself," my friend said sadly, "'Where did we go wrong as parents? What could we have done to prevent this?'"

The myth of prevention

Prevention. It's such a seductive concept. Many of us who should know better believe in the myth of prevention, believe that with the well-timed use of the proper financial, legal, educational, medical, or psychological resources, life's difficulties can always be averted. This is a dangerous kind of magical thinking because, should we reassure ourselves thus when things are going well, we will have to berate ourselves for having failed to take the proper measures when fortune's wheel turns again and things go badly.

Of course I do not mean to imply that we should live our lives without self-control and discipline or that we should treat others heedlessly. Rather, the point is that when troubles do appear, and they always do sooner or later, we are not automatically to blame for having failed to prevent them. In fact, those troubles are often the markers that indicate a change in the direction of our path, just as they were in my friend's family.

She told me in a recent phone conversation that today each of them has an appreciation for what they learned, as individuals and as a family, from that painful period. The boy did spend several months in a foster home before finally deciding that he preferred living within his parents' limits. He returned home and a few months later emerged from his rocky senior year of high school having relinquished his dream of an athletic career, deciding to pursue instead a university degree that would prepare him for a career counseling adolescents. His own difficulties had awakened in him an interest in helping others with similar problems.

During the family therapy sessions in which all four of them had participated, it became apparent to these shocked parents that their daughter was in serious trouble with alcohol, something her younger brother had realized for years but had kept to himself out of loyalty to her. Once her problem was out in the open, treatment became possible. She entered a live-in program for teens with alcohol and drug problems, a program that required family participation.

There her father, in family group sessions, began to address and heal some of his painful childhood experiences with his alcoholic father. And her mother learned to curb her enthusiastic coaching of husband and children, which the family therapist referred to as "managing and controlling." Today my friend is better at allowing those she loves so much to find their own way in their own time.

Thus this young man's teenage rebellion, though extremely trying for those around him while it lasted, initiated a process of self-discovery for each member of the family, a process that will continue throughout their lives.

Struggle is natural to growth

Many years ago when I lived in a small town, the instructor who taught a course called "Senior Problems" at the local high school would ask his young students on the first day of class to anonymously write their answer to the question "At what point in your life so far do you think you changed the most, matured the most?"

His students' responses seldom cited easy, pleasant times such as a summer at camp or a Christmas ski trip, a great day surfing or turning sixteen and getting a car. Instead, each class of seniors gave thoughtful answers such as the following:

"When my parents divorced."
"After my father had his heart attack."
"When my retarded sister was born."
"The year my brother died."
"When our house burned and we lost everything."
"After I found out I had diabetes."

In the discussion that followed, many of the students would talk openly about how these trying times had taught them to be responsible, patient, understanding, compassionate, and appreciative of their blessings.

My son was in this class, and I was surprised when he told me of the wisdom these young people showed. Most of the events to which they attributed their increased maturity were experiences their parents would have tried to spare them, would have prevented if they possibly could have. Does this mean these well-intentioned parents would also have prevented their children from maturing? Possibly, at least temporarily. But if things were too easy, too comfortable for them, these youngsters would have sought out or created other kinds of difficulties against which to struggle. Testing themselves, proving their mettle, and forcing their own growth is a developmental process as natural for adolescents as walking and talking are for toddlers and as natural as designing a lifetime full of challenge is for the soul.

No baby learns to walk without falling or to talk without some difficulty in being understood. If we could prevent every spill and scrape leading to a child's eventual mastery of movement and every error in pronunciation on the way to eventual mastery of language, then we would effectively inhibit that child's ever developing these skills at all. Children can better handle the frustration their own limitations place on them than the frustration produced when they are not allowed to face those limits and overcome them.

However, watching a baby's struggles is made bearable, even enjoyable, because we know the child is learning. We know nothing of the kind regarding a teenager's struggles with sex or drugs or violence. Nor is the outcome predictable regarding most of life's other struggles. Horror stories abound, and we fear for ourselves and those we love. So we try mightily to control, to protect against, to prevent some of the very experiences a soul incarnate may be deliberately seeking or creating.

Addiction as a path to transformation

During the many years I spent working for various nonprofit agencies that offered services in the field of addiction, I learned how much appeal the idea of prevention had for both the general public and for those who monitored our funding. But the longer I worked in the field, the less I believed that prevention of addiction was possible. Such prevention always involved education, approaching the subject as a rational process that could be handled in a rational way. Yet I noticed that some of the very people who had the most information about a subject *manifested addictions in the area of their expertise*. Doctors, nurses, and pharmacists were all too commonly addicted to drugs; nutritionists and dieticians ate compulsively; professionals with careers in banking, accounting, and financial planning spent money compulsively and accrued overwhelming debts; people like myself who counseled others on their relationships were relationship addicts. Again and again the area of expertise fitted together with the addiction to perfectly reflect an inner condition that was in fact a *theme*. I then realized that each of us whose careers and addictions thus meshed were actually dedicated, though we might be unaware of the fact, to exploring that theme in many of its dimensions. Our explorations were, in essence, our life's project.

And finally, as I watched the deep awakening, change, and healing brought about by the various twelve-step programs of recovery, I began to question whether the prevention of addiction was even desirable. Though the stakes were very high and the cost of failure steep indeed, addiction was creating the pressure that made personal transformation possible. This conclusion fit with what I was once told by a man with psychic and healing gifts, whose father had died of alcoholism. He said, "I think addiction offers a person the opportunity to clean up a great deal of karma in one lifetime. But it's always a gamble because recovery requires such a complete and constant surrender of the personal will to a Higher Power. It's a fast track to soul development, but a highly risky one. Often the gamble fails, as it did with my father."

Everything I have observed about addicts, about the addictive process (including experiences with my own relationship addiction), and about recovery leads me to believe he was correct; that the soul sometimes chooses to gamble with addiction because it is the fastest, most efficient means to an end—the end being surrender, awakening, and transformation. When the will cannot be surrendered and the addict fails to recover, other lengthier, more incremental and less drastic healing cycles are options for other lifetimes. Or the soul may gamble with addiction again and again, upping the ante in every subsequent lifetime, increasing the pressure, until that surrender is achieved. Perhaps this is why some of the most saintly recovering alcoholics and addicts are those who were the sickest "skid row" types while they were drinking and using drugs. One has the feeling in the presence of some of these people that theirs is a "resurrection into the Light" after years, even lifetimes, of darkness. And all it took to turn their lives around was the *complete and utter surrender* of their will to a Higher Power.

No wonder then that spouses, children, parents, counselors, ministers, probation officers, or well-meaning friends, no matter how great their efforts, cannot control the addict's practice of the addiction. No one can surrender someone else's will, and therefore no one can bring about anyone else's recovery. Indeed, those of us who would try undoubtedly need to do some surrendering of our own.

For every alcoholic, drug addict, compulsive eater or spender or gambler, there are at least four other people whose lives are completely unmanageable because of their response to the addict's behavior, their unending attempts to control that other person's behavior. Thus addiction provides one of the most potent and far-reaching means through which wide-spread transformation is accomplished, because it involves the entire family, all of whom need to recover and each of whom may thus be transformed. For family members recovery means recognizing one's powerlessness over others, including the addict. Simply recognizing their powerlessness constitutes a transformation in and of itself.

Let me illustrate: When I used to teach on the subject of relationship addiction, at some point during every presentation a mother in the audience would ask me, "How can I prevent my daughter from doing this? She watched me suffer as a relationship addict for years, and she's starting to do a lot of the same things I did. Now that I realize how sick I've been, I want to save her from making all the same mistakes."

My answer was always to ask her simply, "Who could have saved you?"

And then the worried mother and many others in the audience would realize that no one could have kept them from doing exactly as they wished, that whatever positive, growthful changes they had undergone had been brought about precisely *because* of their experiences and their suffering. Anyone preventing their suffering would have precluded their awakening as well.

Often the people attending those classes came to recognize the ways in which interwoven diseases of addiction stretched back over generations in their families, relationship addiction being only one among diseases such as alcoholism, drug addiction, compulsive eating, sexual addiction, etc. Through gaining understanding of their own addictions, they were given the key to understanding generations of previously incomprehensible family dynamics. They were also learning to honor the transformative process as it unfolded in those they loved and not to interfere.

Themes, circles, and family karma

Professionals in the field of addiction have recognized for a while now that wherever there is an addicted individual, there is usually a family history of various interweaving addictions in prior generations. They also understand that this "family disease" of addiction will continue to develop in succeeding generations unless treated. The clinical explanation is that inherited genetic factors predispose family members to substance dependency, just as their progenitors were predisposed to such dependencies. This genetic factor, coupled with the emotional and behavioral conditioning operating in a family where addiction is a theme, virtually guarantees that some form of addiction will be present in succeeding generations.

Although we understand the soul may choose parents who present us with difficulties, you may ask yourself, as I did during my years of working in the field of substance abuse: "What unkind Force would cause a child to be born to parents suffering from addiction, given the fact that most incidents of physical battering and sexual abuse occur in addicted families?"

In the face of such indifference to the welfare of the incarnating being, we would almost have to conclude there was no God at all, no Power for love in the Universe, *unless such conditions and circumstances were freely chosen by the incarnating being* for the purpose of:

EXPRESSION · EXPERIENCE · EXPANSION

Then and only then would it seem to be a just world in which there was meaning and order and hope of true progress.

What if, for instance, the daughter of the relationship-addicted mother *chose* to be born into a family where relationship addiction would be an issue? What if, indeed, the presence of that issue was one of the *key* factors in that daughter's decision to incarnate, specifically drawing her to this particular mother and to the field in which relationship addiction and other addictions as well could be explored? Taking this concept to its next logical level, what if this mother, this daughter, and others with whom they each are linked through ties of matrimony, family, and friendship have, in other lifetimes, had many different relationships with each other while addiction remained, throughout, the central conditioning theme in all their interactions? Those persons who together conduct such an exploration over many lifetimes constitute a *circle*. Every such circle is an expression of family and group karmas in operation, embodying the evolutionary processes of expression, experience, and expansion organized around a specific and shared theme. When we incarnate within such circles, it is in order to explore a theme's different facets and eventually achieve balance in our understanding of that issue.

These explorations within circles take place in much the same way whether we are considering how several generations of family members go about their interwoven tasks or how one individual incarnating several times does so. This may become clear for you in the next example.

Three generations of family karma

In the following story Christa, her mother, and her daughter, Lindsey, form a family circle through which the themes of alcoholism, coalcoholism, and suicide interweave. Christa, in particular, illustrates how the same person can play different roles and experience different aspects of the explored issue at different points along the way in just one lifetime. Through her interactions first as a child with her mother and then later as a parent to her daughter, she develops greater understanding of some of the many facets of addiction, depression, and suicide. It is the necessary repetition of these themes generation after generation that brings this understanding about.

I was fourteen when my mom killed herself with pills and alcohol. When I came home from school that day she was in bed, but that was nothing new. Whenever my dad was away on business, my mom drank alone in her room while I tiptoed around the house, trying not to wake her or upset her. It was way past dinnertime when I finally went in to make sure she was okay, leaving the light off to keep from hurting her eyes. I kept saying, "Mom . . . Mom . . . ," afraid to bother her but afraid, too, that something might be wrong. Finally I touched her and that's how I knew, all alone there in the dark, that my mother was dead.

When I turned on the light I saw the note she'd left. All it said was "Please forgive me." Well, I couldn't. Not then and not for a long, long time afterward. I don't think I ever would have, except I ended up the same way myself.

Everything changed pretty fast after she died. First my dad and I moved to another part of the state, and I went to a new school where nobody knew what my mom had done. Then my dad got married again after only a few months to a woman who had two daughters a few years younger than I was. None of them ever talked about what had happened before. It was as though they all wanted to pretend that my mom had never existed, and instead there was this instant, *awful* family, and we were all supposed to be really happy. Well, I hated them all, especially my dad, who was constantly telling me in a whisper how lucky I was, how grateful I should be. The situation had been bad with my mom, but this was worse. I was pretty sure this was my punishment for letting her die. Even today, when anything really goes wrong, really hurts, I still feel that way.

I started sneaking alcohol myself, adding water to replace what I'd drunk from their supply. I felt good about ripping them off, like I was doing it for my mom somehow, getting back at all of them for acting like she'd never lived or died.

By sixteen I was pretty wild. By nineteen I was married to a stuntman twice my age. By twenty-five I had a good job as a hairdresser at one of the network studios. My husband and I drank a lot, partied a lot. Every year he worked less and I worked more to make up the difference. By thirty-two my increasingly frequent blackouts drove me to get help in AA, and after I was clean and sober six months, my husband told me he wanted a divorce; he was in love with someone else. For years we hadn't had much in common except drinking together, and when I got sober we didn't even have that. In a way I didn't blame him for leaving.

After he moved out things were difficult but not impossible. I had my work, my twelve-year-old daughter, Lindsey, my AA meetings, and my sponsor to keep me going. But two years into sobriety I began to battle a depression that wouldn't let go. I had to take off work and stay in bed because I was unable to function. My mind went a thousand miles an hour telling me what a terrible person I was, what a failure—yet I could barely talk or move. It was like trying to swim in wet cement. Everything took so much effort.

Lindsey would come home from school and there I'd be, in bed, just wanting to be left alone. Even though I wasn't drinking, I was acting just like my mother had, and Lindsey was responding exactly as I had at her age. She tried not to upset me, took over lots of my chores, fought with me occasionally, but mostly she kept trying to make things better. I had terrible guilt about what was happening, what I was doing to her, but I couldn't turn it around. I began to see suicide as the only way out. Even my horror at the thought of putting Lindsey through what I suffered at her age only fed my sense of worthlessness and the conviction that the world, my daughter, everybody would be better off without me.

My AA sponsor was the one who got me through it. She welcomed my calls at any hour of the day or night, and many, many nights just knowing I *could* call her kept me from having to. I prayed. I worked the steps of the program. I accepted love and support from others in AA, even when I was sure I didn't deserve it. And finally, after nearly a year and a half, the depression started to lift. First I'd have a good hour, then a good day. Then a couple of good days in a row, and then a whole week. It was like something was slowly letting the light back in where there'd been nothing but darkness.

For a long time I expected the depression to take hold again, but it hasn't yet. Oh, I've had bad days, but no bad weeks, and it's been four years now.

I've thought a lot about my mother's alcoholism and suicide and the way I followed in her footsteps, what I put my daughter through when I would have given anything not to do that to her. Lindsey and I have talked about it a lot, and I've done my best to make amends to her. But I know today that I was as powerless over that depression as I am over my alcoholism. Without the help of the program, I wouldn't have made it.

My mother never had that help, so how can I judge her?

If addiction or suicide or any other major issue is something we experience in one lifetime but don't resolve, we are likely to join a circle in which that theme is explored in other incarnations. It is very possible that for Christa, suicide was an unresolved issue from at least one other lifetime. In order to better understand that act and forgive it *while incarnate*, she had to face the situation again. She chose a mother whose alcoholism and potential for suicide set her up to do so. Then, at approximately the age her mother was when she took her life, and with a daughter the age Christa was back when it happened, Christa was under the compelling influence of the most powerful anniversary of her life. Further, she was caught in a triple identification, in a way responding as three different people to this anniversary.

First, she felt she had become her own mother, so full of despair that she wasn't able to put her daughter's well-being ahead of her desire to end her anguish. Second, she identified strongly with Lindsey, reliving the anguish she, too, had known at that age when forced to cope alone with a sick, suicidal parent. Third, she was herself, an adult overcome with depression and the urge to end her life. Christa was, in effect, undergoing three crises simultaneously, all related to suicide. It was a terrible time, and when it was finally over her understanding allowed her to forgive her mother. In doing so, I have no doubt she forgave herself as well for the same act in another lifetime.

Lindsey's exposure to a parent's alcoholism and near suicide was greatly tempered by her mother's recovering from alcoholism and later from depression. Through Christa's example, Lindsey is at least aware that tools exist with which to address whatever form these themes take in her own life.

If Lindsey, too, develops problems similar to her mother's and grandmother's, and if her children and their children do so as well, where, you may ask, does it end? By recognizing that there are several karmas operating, you will be better able to answer that question. First, there is each individual's karma. Christa's likely history of choosing suicide as an answer to challenges presented while incarnate required that she face such a decision again and choose otherwise. There is also the family karma, comprised of relationships conditioned by these recurring themes of alcoholism, depression, and suicide. Their shared karmic task was to elevate their reactions from a level of blaming and condemnation to greater understanding and forgiveness.

This family's story illustrates how, in the thematic context of the family or the wider group, we incarnate and gain experience, then knowledge, and finally wisdom. Love that comes from deep understanding completes our karma. We have experienced a condition, learned from it, and healed it. Now we are free to go on to other lessons. Still we may continue to incarnate around the same themes and with others in the same circle in order to teach them, to help them heal, to bring needed light and love to bear on their condition. Such an incarnation is a demonstration of the law of sacrifice and applies to healing the family or the larger group. In all existence there are wider and wider karmas, that, like individual karmas, must be addressed and healed.

Our contribution to the body of humanity

It is not my intention here to address the subjects of racial, national, and planetary karmas. However, their existence in addition to personal, family, and group karmas must at least be noted because each of us, as members of these larger groups, is subject to vast and impersonal forces that profoundly affect our individual lives. Nevertheless, to understand the concepts of family and group karma we must accept that, in addition to being separate individuals, we are also joined together with others with whom we comprise contributing units in the great body of humanity, *which is a living being in its own right.*

Our own physical body provides an analogy. We know that various individual cells in combination with others similar to themselves make up organs with separate yet interdependent tasks, all vital to the overall development and maintenance of the physical body. In much the same way, individual people, in combination with others genetically similar to themselves (their family) and with shared interests (their group), make up units or circles with separate yet interdependent tasks all vitally necessary to the development of humanity.

Whatever we accomplish as individuals on behalf of the body of humanity is usually done either through close and harmonious cooperation *with* or in more or less violent reaction *against* others within our circle and with whom we share family or group karma. Much of our trouble with others in a given lifetime arises from the fact that, bound together as we are, we force one another to experience different, even opposing dimensions of related issues.

Along with the situational challenges we present to one another, the spiritual challenges are always there as well. A cold, indifferent mother may force us to abandon our dependence and need for approval and learn to stand on our own, which may be an important requisite for some other task we are here to undertake in this lifetime. Thus that unloving mother actually becomes one of the means by which we are able to achieve our goal. Or in our search for approval from a disapproving parent we may take on challenges we wouldn't accept otherwise, until one day we realize what incredible things we've accomplished. Perhaps we have a subtly cruel mother or father who helps to create in us a sensitive awareness of how easily pain can be inflicted through a few words, a look, or a gesture. As in the case of George, such a parent can create in us an aversion for cruelty, helping us to consciously overcome the same tendency in ourselves. Most of us have had the experience of deciding to be very different from a parent in certain aspects and then finding, in spite of our resolution, that the same traits are indeed unfolding in ourselves and must be overcome. And so our parent has helped awaken us to our task.

Certainly there are from some parents the welcome gifts of love, but there are from others the less welcome gifts of hate and weakness and addiction and poverty and betrayal and abasement, all providing us with the opportunity to redeem our own character defects. For our spiritual development we need our enemies and our afflictions as foils against which to test ourselves in order that we may become all we are capable of being.

Shared karmic tasks

Of course we forget, while struggling with the overwhelming responsibility we feel for our alcoholic mother or the social embarrassment we experience because of our retarded sibling or the revenge fantasies we harbor toward our violent father, or the helpless rage engendered by our sexist employer or our increasingly obsessive efforts to control our philandering spouse, that these difficulties are the areas of learning we *chose* to address in this incarnation, the fields of study to which our soul was attracted for our present sojourn in the school of life. A daughter who incarnates with a mission to advance understanding of the dynamics of violence may *require* a brutal father to provide her with the necessary field of experience. Nor would this be her mission unless she was seeking to further her own expression, experience, and expansion on the theme of violence. Indeed, there may exist between her and her father an ancient karmic debt that will be laid to rest should she use his treatment of her as the springboard to her own deeper understanding and healing. And if she eventually uses that healing to help others similarly abused, so much the better. Can you see how, should this happen, both she and her father have, *together*, become instruments for healing? Their contrasting contributions are necessary in order to complete the task that, at a soul level, they agreed to address together.

Sometimes people share a karmic task that they can accomplish precisely by not getting along. Often such a task involves serving others, revealing a truth, founding a needed institution or movement, or doing something else that affects others beyond those persons immediately involved. Interestingly, these incarnational dynamics can frequently be discerned or verified when the horoscopes of the people involved are read and compared by a skilled and sensitive astrologer. Often, in the case of the most difficult relationships between family members, their two charts, when compared, seem together to make one complete picture, indicating that they share such a joint karmic task. This is the case with the women whose story follows.

Helen and Lydia have been battling all their lives. Helen, the older sister, is tall, dark haired and voluptuous, given to wearing gaudy clothes and driving flashy cars. She is outspoken and demanding and almost always gets her way. Lydia, two years younger, is also tall and dark, but doe eyed and ethereal, with an other-worldly air about her. But in her quiet, self-effacing way, Lydia has fully as much determination as her sister Helen.

When their parents divorced because of the father's drinking and infidelity and the mother's fierce temper, the girls were seven and nine. Helen spent as much time as she could with their free-spending, alcoholic, playboy father, while Lydia remained loyally devoted to their exotic, emotional, superstitious, and financially canny Greek mother. When their mother died in her fifties, the two daughters were bound to one another financially through their joint inheritance of their mother's properties.

At sixteen, Helen had run off with an older man who,

just before the birth of their son, Michael, reunited with his former wife. When baby Michael arrived Helen's mother had been furious with her and her father had been drunk, as usual. Only fourteen-year-old Lydia had come to the hospital to visit her sister and her new nephew.

With nowhere else to go, Helen had brought the baby home to her mother's house where, for months, her angry mother had refused to speak to her. Helen worked nights to support herself and the baby. Her mother worked days. Lydia went to school, and the two sisters divided the baby's care between them. Although both sisters adored the baby, right from the beginning they had totally different viewpoints regarding his needs and welfare—and each believed the other was doing everything wrong. Helen, at least partly from a practical standpoint, insisted that Michael's feedings follow a strict schedule. She would wake him from a nap in order to feed him on time. But when Lydia was in charge of the baby's care, feedings were on demand rather than on schedule, a situation that often played havoc with Helen's attempts to get some sleep during the day and get to work on time in the evenings.

Years passed. Helen remarried but had no more children. Lydia never married, quietly living at home with her mother until her mother died and always remaining as close to Michael as her difficult relationship with Helen would allow. In his midtwenties Michael was diagnosed with myelocytic leukemia, a deadly cancer that usually kills its victims within three or four years.

From the moment Michael's illness was identified, his mother and his aunt argued furiously over the correct approach to treatment for this young man so dear to both of them. Helen was a natural-born fighter and regarded her son's illness as a bitter foe to be battled with every medical means possible. When Michael began radiation treatment and chemotherapy, neither of which is very successful with this kind of cancer, Lydia was appalled. She believed these treatments weakened the immune system and urged Michael to explore alternative approaches—a healer, meditation, herbs, and diet. Her advocacy of these nontraditional approaches enraged Helen, who saw her as undermining the doctor's authority.

Michael quietly combined Lydia's recommendations with the doctor's and stabilized for a while. But when after a year and a half he began to decline rapidly, each sister held the other to blame.

As his suffering increased, Lydia tried to talk Helen out of continuing to pursue every possible medical gambit, many of which were both painful and exhausting. She wanted Michael out of the hospital and at home. Lydia had been through the dying process with two friends and knew what a beautiful, peaceful passage it could be. With her strong belief in an afterlife and reincarnation, she felt sure the kindest, most loving thing for Michael now was to keep him comfortable and help him let go. Helen simply regarded her sister as a dangerous traitor and insisted that her son stay in the hospital where any necessary emergency measures could be taken to keep Michael alive. Even after Michael went into a coma, Helen went right on fighting, exhorting the doctor to *do* something, convinced that to let him die was a terrible betrayal of her son.

So Helen battled and Lydia prayed and Michael slowly slipped away. By the time he died, both women had learned a great deal about the many dimensions of cancer, and both were deeply involved, each in her own very different way, in educating the community and developing resources for those battling the disease in its many forms.

Today both these women contribute so vitally to the local network of services for those with cancer that it is difficult for anyone affiliated with that network to imagine its functioning without them. Helen is organizing fund-raisers to finance new equipment, ramrodding through red tape to secure medical services for needy patients, and promoting support services for families and friends. In contrast to Helen's high-profile activities, Lydia silently offers her own deep acceptance of the process of dying to patients in the last stages of their illness. Completely present and available to them as they make their transition, she honors their right to die as fully as her sister battles for their right to live.

Now these two sisters are in the process of converting one of the pieces of property they jointly inherited from their mother into a vitally needed care facility for those with cancer. No doubt Helen and Lydia will battle their way through this new endeavor, just as they always have with every other task they've shared. The deep love each holds for Michael, to whom this new facility will be dedicated, keeps them from splintering apart. Each has a will of iron. Each has deep integrity. Neither can be swayed off course. And though they rail at each other and suffer from feeling misunderstood and unappreciated, the work they accomplish in tandem has a curious balance and completeness.

Sharing a karmic task as Helen and Lydia do is rarely easy or comfortable, because it so often is the very friction generated between or among those involved that makes accomplishment possible. Consider now your own most trying family relations, the persons with whom you share blood ties and quite possibly karmic tasks as well. If you were able to appreciate that Helen and Lydia, with their very different natures and perspectives, were nevertheless both sincere, try to bring that same objectivity to your consideration of those with whom you are bound.

Imagine what you and the relatives with whom you struggle may very well be accomplishing together. See the ways you have all grown and stretched and expanded because of the pressures generated among you. Or perhaps you as an individual have become more fixedly true to yourself in reaction to whoever in your family has been your greatest nemesis. Seek the balance that your combined natures may strike. Look for the lessons to your own soul and the gifts to the larger group that this bond may be generating. Let this expanded perspective of the nature of your family ties linger in your consciousness, and you will eventually come to appreciate *as necessary* the very qualities and behaviors in others that you have previously resented most deeply.

Will you, like an alchemist striving to extract gold from base metals, search for that which is precious among the dreariest and most discouraging aspects of your life? If you do you will find it there, awaiting your conscious discovery.

Seven

Where Am I Going and When Will I Get There?

Fairy tales . . . myths . . . epic sagas of daring deeds performed by courageous adventurers . . .

These familiar and beloved stories, with all their fantastic and magical details, cast their spell over us again and again, generation after generation. Regardless of the circumstances of our lives they speak to us, draw us in, carry us along because they are, in fact, *our* story. Through symbolic metaphors they describe you and me and our heroic quest—a journey in which first we are separated from our Source, then forced to expand through experience, to overcome temptation, dispel illusion, and conquer our character defects until we finally return home enlightened.

Such stories often begin by introducing an unexceptional or even foolish youth such as Jack in "Jack and the Beanstalk," or else a young nobleman who must nevertheless prove his mettle. Very often he is the youngest and therefore the most innocent of three brothers, naive and blessed with bright optimism. Much like the Fool whose unnumbered card in the tarot deck indicates endless possibilities (all, however, requiring work), our protagonist leaves home to make his way in the world and seek his fortune.

Often he begins his quest in order to help his father in some way, just as we incarnate to help our soul expand. In the favorite Russian fairy tale "The Firebird," the youngest son of the king, Prince Ivan, leaves home in search of the Firebird, who has stolen golden apples from his father's orchard. Like most protagonists in such stories—and like most beings incarnate—his quest begins in a straightforward enough manner, but soon his actions embroil him in a series of hazardous adventures. The prince comes to a crossroads marked by a stone inscribed "Straight ahead to find a wife, turn left and be killed and turn right to lose your horse." Thinking it is too early to find a wife and not wanting to die, he turns right. Later, awakening from a nap, he finds his horse gone. A gray wolf admits to killing his horse and eating it but offers to take its place, carrying the prince on his back and acting as his faithful servant.

The wolf takes the prince to where the Firebird is, warning him to take only the bird but not its golden cage. Prince Ivan cannot resist the cage, an alarm is sounded, and he is caught. The king who owns the Firebird demands that in return for his freedom, the Firebird, and the cage, the prince must bring him the horse with the golden mane. The prince's dilemma parallels what happens as the soul makes its way through the perils of incarnation. Each necessary experience inevitably creates consequences or karma that must be dealt with, and for a long and weary while there are furious battles in dangerous regions, challenging difficulties that must be conquered if the incarnating part of the soul, like the vagabond in our tale, is ever to return home.

Now Prince Ivan goes off to find the horse, warned by the wolf to take only the horse, not its golden bridle. But the prince cannot resist the bridle, an alarm is raised, and the angry king who owns the horse demands of the prince that in return for his freedom and the horse and its golden bridle as well, Ivan bring him Fair Helen for his bride.

Every such challenge compares to the energetic price paid for the soul's experiences on the Earth plane. These experiences produce consequences, karma that, like the task confronting our prince, must be faced and overcome or all progress is halted. Many attempts on Prince Ivan's part, many lifetimes on the part of the soul, may be necessary before these challenges are overcome.

In most mythic tales our protagonist is tempted and trapped and challenged, meeting and overcoming various difficulties and thereby gaining experience, confidence, and maturity until he has developed into a hero indeed, a veritable superman. But as his powers increase, so does his reckless hubris. At the peak of his strength he falls into a trap or is wounded in such a way that not even his immense strength and courage can save him. He has achieved so much, overcome so much, only to find himself utterly powerless. Such is the case with Prince Ivan. Having stolen not only the Firebird but the horse and Fair Helen as well, he thanks the wolf for all his help, ignoring the wolf's warning that he may need further help still. Smugly confident, he decides to pause on the way home and rest. As he and Fair Helen are sleeping, his two brothers, passing by and seeing him with the Firebird, the horse with the golden mane, and Fair Helen, decide to kill him, one taking the horse and the Firebird and the other, Fair Helen.

Prince Ivan lies dead on the plain ninety days before the wolf sees his body and bribes a crow to bring him the waters of death and life. With the waters of death he heals the prince's wounds. With the waters of life he revives him. "But for me," says the wolf, "you would have slept forever."

And so the wolf, that powerful being that has accompanied the hero from the beginning of his journey to its end—watching over him, guiding him, allowing him to be chastened and tempered by defeat, and then restoring him to wholeness—now brings him home to his father's house with those treasures that are the gifts of his quest.

All such stories describe our journey through incarnation on the Earth plane under the soul's guidance. Esoterically and mystically the soul is regarded as feminine. The marriage of the hero to the beautiful maiden or princess signifies completion of the cycle by uniting the seeker with the soul. This perfect union of masculine and feminine is depicted by the dancing hermaphrodite on the last card of the tarot entitled the World. This card represents the end of the Fool's journey through Life, the final achievement of perfect unity.

From naive innocence through tests of courage to final wisdom and perfection, the hero's journey is our journey. Little wonder, then, that no matter how often we hear these timeless tales, we never tire of the brave wayfarer, who after perilous expeditions into far-off lands where enemies were conquered, damsels were wooed, and battles were lost and won, finally, victoriously, comes home.

We are ambassadors for the soul

If during our day-to-day existence we see ourselves less as inde-
fatigable crusaders on an immense quest and more as tired play-
ers in an endless soap opera, it is because our vision is restricted.
During an Earth-plane incarnation, we identify almost completely with our physical body and its sense perceptions, to which
our personality adds its interpretations of reality. We are unaware
that taken together, these merely comprise the soul's outpost in
the dense physical plane. Our overidentification with our vehicle
for physical existence is roughly analogous to deciding to make a
journey, finding a car, and driving it in the direction of our destination but believing only in the reality of the vehicle, the road,
the scenery, and events along the way—completely forgetting
that *we* have chosen to make the trip, *we* are driving there, and *we*
will finally arrive. The input from our physical senses obscures
the fact that the soul that sends us forth is a greater reality than
is our temporary vehicle for the journey.

As an ambassador for the soul on the Earth plane, a human
being incarnate is moving in one of two directions. Like our hero,
we are either traveling away from home or, having learned much
from our journey, we are returning. Esoterically it is said we are
either on the Outward Path or the Path of Return. While on the
Outward Path, we are descending into physical matter and are
becoming more and more closely identified with it, first through
our physical body and the sensations and experiences with which
it provides us, and then through our understanding of ourselves
as a personality, a force for realizing our desires in the material
world. On the Path of Return we are drawn back toward our orig-

inating Source, carrying with us all we have gained through our adventures. However, as we have seen before, in order to be reconciled with that which sent us forth, we must release whatever karma we have generated and heal whatever wounds we bear as a consequence of those experiences undergone on the Outward Path. Most of these wounds and their accompanying frozen configurations of energy or "energetic scars" are released through understanding, forgiveness, and remediation through service.

Human development from birth to death

This entire process of moving outward and returning home is demonstrated in microcosm in the development of a human being during a single lifetime. We are born and spend the earliest period of our life primarily focused on mastering our physical vehicle. As we gain greater mastery, our attention is transferred increasingly to the larger world with all its enticements, opportunities, and challenges. We feel the power of our developing personality and begin to make decisions, take action. As consequences unfold, we gain experience. The process, however, takes its toll on us. Bumps and bruises and some profound wounds, too, occur along the way, both to our physical body and, even more important, to the deeper levels where our emotions and thoughts dwell. These bumps and bruises and wounds are an inevitable and even necessary part of life's experience, a rich source of learning and understanding and growth. But their accompanying pain and scarring always cause some degree of impairment or even crippling to those areas of us that are affected. Whatever impairment we sustain—whether physical, emotional, or mental—unless healed, tends to persist for the duration of our lifetime, often causing us to grow more rigid, more fixed and frozen with time.

In later life there comes a point of reorientation. As our physical body begins to fail, the outer world's pull on us lessens. More and more there is a turning inward or, if you will, upward. What are usually referred to as spiritual concerns begin to occupy us. A deep need often emerges to make sense of our life and also to clean up some of the loose ends, to heal long-standing feuds and breaches, to shed old grudges and affect reconciliations. Replacing our former appetite for more and wider experience is a yearning for peace, both inner and outer, and a willingness to release whatever stands in the way of that peace, including, finally, the physical body.

Soul development throughout many lifetimes

This concept of progressive unfoldment as we move outward into more potent physical manifestation and then, at a point of rich maturity, reverse back toward our center and source can also accommodate the macrocosmic concept of multiple lives experienced on behalf of the soul.

The soul's progress through innumerable incarnations follows a pattern similar to that of individual human development, beginning with a long period during which gaining mastery over the physical vehicle or body is its principle work. This mastery, when achieved after many lifetimes, is followed by development and refinement first of the emotional equipment, then of the mental apparatus. The next goal of incarnation, again requiring many lifetimes, is the successful coordination of all these elements: the physical, emotional, and mental aspects (or bodies). When these

bodies are finally aligned and functioning in energetic synchronization, a truly integrated personality is the result.

The integrated personality, once achieved, is a potent vehicle
for expression in the outer world, a powerful force *for good or
for evil*. It is precisely at this point of development that the soul
begins to take greater notice of its manifestation on the Earth
plane. At long last the soul has, in the integrated personality, a
vehicle sufficiently evolved so as to be capable of expressing in
material existence the soul's qualities. And so the soul begins to
call to its manifestation, to make its claim upon its vehicle of
expression.

What happens next parallels a parent calling a child in from
play just when the child is swept away by the glorious part he is
enacting in a make-believe drama. At first the child will fail to
even hear the parent's call, so strong is the magical spell he is
under, and when the adult voice is finally heard, the child resents
the intrusion and resists the summons. Stronger measures are
necessary if the child is to be persuaded to come home.

The case is much the same when the soul calls to the integrated personality, which in the full flush of Earth-plane potency,
resists and resents the claim. A struggle between the personality
and the soul ensues. There follows a succession of lives in which
the pressure of suffering, generated by flaws in our own character, finally brings about a recognition of the limitations of our
self-obsession, selfishness, and self-will. When Prince Ivan dis-
missed the wolf, deciding he was strong enough and clever enough
to complete the journey on his own, he suffered the worst catastrophe of all. He was slain and lay dead for a long time. Only the
wolf's attentions and ministrations could awaken him and carry
him home.

All of us must eventually learn that we cannot make our journey alone. From great and sometimes terrible pressures, our personality develops the willingness to surrender to a power higher and greater than itself. When we do so, our gradual or sudden healing from those difficulties that brought about our surrender follows.

We are increasingly aware of our soul's guidance as we begin to tread the Path of Return. Incompleted episodes from previous lifetimes from which we still bear wounds and scars are repeated, now reappearing as healing cycles. Pressures are generated and we are tested and tried. Eventually we surrender to these healing cycles: understanding, forgiveness, and service are the result.

The more we meet and overcome old karma, heal old wounds, and release old scars, the stronger and more conscious our identification with our soul becomes. Through innumerable lifetimes we develop an ever finer and more sensitive vehicle for soul expression until finally the division between that which manifests in matter and that which sent it forth into manifestation dissolves. "At-onement" between the soul and its vehicle is achieved. It is not a coincidence that *atonement*, meaning remediation, and *At-onement*, describing our reconciliation with our soul, are essentially the same word. As we will see later in this chapter, atonement (remediation) is the final step in that reconciliation.

Young souls and old souls

The journey away from our Source and back again is a long process of stages and cycles, each different from the others. Just as a youth and a mature person will doubtless take different approaches to the same problem, so a so-called "young soul" on the

Outward Path and an "old soul" on the Path of Return will react to similar situations and conditions in markedly different ways. As a younger soul seeking the needed experience, we will often tend to initiate and perpetuate difficulties through a combative stance or a dogged determination to prevail. This is exactly as it should be, as we are developing physical courage and personal integrity and exercising these for their own sake, learning to stand up for ourselves and fight those in our way. There is a heavy emphasis on "I, me, my." What we seek to achieve is first of all for our personal self, then later this sphere may extend to *my* wife, *my* children, *my* family, *my* community, *my* country. We exercise power and influence for their own sake and for personal gain. We may make heroically courageous soldiers but get into trouble with the law as civilians because of our aggressive reactions to those who oppose us. This self-absorbed perspective regarding how our personal life is affected, whether the issue is nuclear armament or the neighbor's barking dog, is entirely appropriate on the Outward Path and paves the way for all subsequent development. After all, in order to practice true moral courage, we must have already developed physical courage. And, in terms of psychological development, there must first *be* an ego before the ego can be transcended.

Our life is a very different affair when we are on the Outward Path than it is while we are nearing the Point of Integration, and it is different still as we advance along the Path of Return. No matter what our outer circumstances may be, at the early stages of the journey, our life is a chaotic and dramatic adventure, evoking strong physical and emotional reactions of all kinds. Mastering our physical body—enhancing its strength and perfecting its abilities—is a common concern. But we have far less conscious control of our emotions than we will have at a later point on the Path. Because our mental abilities are not yet well developed, we are usually happier when involved in physical tasks than intellectual pursuits.

By the time the Point of Integration is reached, life is no longer lived through reaction but rather through action achieved using rational thinking and conscious control. We have developed our ability to conceive goals and bring them to fruition through deliberate planning. We are gaining ascendency in life; we feel our power and are intoxicated by it.

Acknowledgment is very important to us at this stage of our evolvement. It is at the Point of Integration that we are most likely to be recognized for our power, our achievements, and our influence. The majority of those we read about—politicians, members of the entertainment industry, leaders of movements— are at the Point of Integration, exercising their great power for good or for ill. In the strong personality that characterizes someone at the Point of Integration, two traits are universally present: *self-will* and *self-obsession*. Self-will is the conviction that our view is the right one, accompanied by great determination to achieve our ends. Self-obsession is a preoccupation with our own uniqueness and a demand that this uniqueness be noted and appreciated by others. Often it is this demand to be recognized as special by our fellows that eventually leads us into the very tests and trials that finally reconcile us with our soul. And as we gradually yield our self-will and self-obsession, we turn the evolutionary corner and begin to tread the Path of Return.

Once the soul's claim is finally heard and heeded, all the rules for living change. Having internalized through great effort rules and guidelines for successful living, we now find they no longer serve us. This is because on the Path of Return our task is no longer to develop physical courage as it was on the Outward Path, or to think and plan and wield power as it was at the Point of Integration. Instead of working to achieve the personality's goals, now we must courageously and thoughtfully use our power to serve the group, guided by conscious contact with a Higher Power.

On the Path of Return we face just as many if not more challenges, both outer and inner, but now the resolution of every issue, every problem demands a solution that takes into account the welfare of *all*, not just our own welfare or even that of our personal group. As we identify with all of humanity, our emphasis shifts toward greater inclusiveness, seeing all sides, taking no dogmatic positions for or against, no matter how noble the cause. We become willing to yield, to understand, to forgive, and above all to serve. What are now important are the goals of the soul rather than the personality.

A formula for the entire process of human evolution, from the Outer Path to the Point of Integration and then onto the Path of Return, could be stated thus:

Lack of Control → Conscious Control → Conscious Surrender

or

Reacting to Life → Acting in Life → Serving Life

To a person at one point on the Path, the values, beliefs, and actions of another person at a different point may seem incomprehensible, even indefensible. However, once a person is sufficiently advanced on the Path of Return (a point very, very few have reached), true tolerance is achieved. Just as the adult accepts that the child's understanding and capabilities are limited by lack of development, so the person at an advanced point on the Path of Return respects and honors the attitudes and behaviors of those fellow travelers who have not yet journeyed as far through as many lifetimes.

How consciousness expands through experience

Only a being of the highest spiritual development is capable of seeing with understanding his Path through many lifetimes. It is said that the Buddha at His final enlightenment saw clearly every one of His lifetimes on Earth and understood the contribution of each. When we achieve the consciousness we came here to develop, then we, too, will review all our lifetimes at once.

Meanwhile we tend to believe, because of our necessarily limited perspective, that this one life of which we are aware—this one we are currently living—is who and what we are in entirety. But very occasionally we come upon intimations that a far larger picture does indeed exist, one to which we've already contributed much and which has, in turn, influenced the kind of life we're now living.

The following story illuminates one woman's unfolding understanding and progress along the Path through succeeding lifetimes. She is a horse trainer I'll call Paula, a woman who, rather than adopting the frequently cruel methods commonly used in her profession, has earned admiration and respect through her consistently humane approach. She uses gentle touching and reassurance with every animal she encounters, no matter how challenging its behavior, tuning into its unique character and capabilities and taking into consideration any possible history of trauma. Some of the results she achieves verge on the miraculous. We met when I attended a demonstration she conducted, and during a conversation together afterward she told me the remarkable story that follows.

This happened about six months ago. I had just finished lecturing to a large crowd when a woman approached me, introduced herself as Anna, and handed me a folded piece of paper, asking me to please read it later in private. I thanked her, put the note in my coat pocket, and promptly forgot all about it until weeks later when I put the same coat on again. In the note Anna identified herself as a psychic and went on to write that during the lecture she had seen a large man in Regency clothing appear on the stage with me, standing slightly behind me and to my left. Anna identified him as one of my Guides who had himself been me in another lifetime.

Watching him while I was speaking, Anna said she saw scenes from his life and then the circumstances of his death. He, too, had been a horse trainer, one who was particularly brutal in his methods and who frequently vented his anger on his horses. He had died after a horse kicked him, striking him in the back in the area of the left kidney. His dying had been long and slow and excruciatingly painful, and there had been much time to consider his own misery and the misery he had inflicted.

Anna wrote that through this suffering he had burned off at least some of the karma he had generated during that inhumane lifetime. She suggested that I might have either had a scarring accident in that same area of my back in this lifetime or been born with some kind of birthmark there.

When I read that note, I immediately *knew* everything this woman had written was true. I knew that Regency man's experiences, and I knew that he was a part of me now, prompting me to use better methods in this lifetime. Maybe the most amazing part of all is that I do have a large red birthmark on my back in the area of my left kidney!

Often, as in Paula's case, there is physical evidence in the way of scars, birthmarks, deformities, or weaknesses related to trauma in past lives. Often, too, subsequent lifetimes reveal the incremental process of evolution in consciousness. Imagine, for instance, that prior to Paula's incarnation as the Regency-era horse trainer, she had many lifetimes of involvement with horses, including one in which she lost someone beloved, owing to an accident caused by the capriciousness of a horse. The pain of that loss caused her anger and anguish to freeze into place. Following that lifetime was another as the Regency-era trainer, who took revenge through brutal training methods designed to stamp out all such capriciousness, producing animals so wearied by punishment that they were only broken automatons.

The cruel trainer, dying, underwent an awakening brought about by the injury, which was a direct result of his inhumanity. This awakening to the misery he had inflicted was a result of his own personal experience of physical suffering, combined with the evolution of his consciousness.

Such an awakening may occur while the being is still in the physical body, or it may happen during the "postmortem review" (a phrase coined by Kenneth Ring, who has studied the near-death experience extensively). Remember, during the postmortem review the events and experiences of the just completed incarnation are seen with a clarity, objectivity, and coherence impossible while we are in the physical body and influenced by the personality. This postmortem review always brings about an expansion in consciousness. Bringing that expansion into personal awareness during physical incarnation is the soul's ongoing task, working as it must within the limitations of time, space, and physical matter.

As much as we may deplore cruelty and resist suffering, it is important to remember that all these experiences are necessary, because while on the Earth plane we learn and we become conscious through *contrast*, through *duality*, through experiencing opposing states of being. We are usually only aware of our health, for instance, if illness has recently been a part of our experience. We will take abundance for granted unless we have known deprivation. And cruel behavior may not seem so until compared with expressions of kindness and compassion. Until our consciousness evolves, we react to our own suffering with a desire for revenge or retribution. But as we develop the capacity to feel others' suffering as well as our own, there is awakened in us, as in the Regency-era horse trainer reborn as Paula, a reversed dedication to relieve that suffering rather than inflict it.

As the brutal trainer, Paula was ruled by her emotions, especially the desire for revenge. This is indicative of someone still on the Outward Path. Today she is healing old karma generated during that previous lifetime, serving animals and teaching those who care for them her gentle methods of training. There may have been many incarnations between that long-ago lifetime of cruelty and the present, during which Paula evolved through the Point of Integration. But her present life of dedicated service is indicative of a person on the Path of Return.

Karma, remediation, and the wounded healer

Our first task on the Path of Return is *remediation* for whatever karma has been generated in the long process of deepening our consciousness. At the highest level of remediation we oppose nothing; we only help. In Paula's case, for instance, in order for remediation to occur there must be as much compassion for those human beings whose fear or ignorance leads either to inadvertent or deliberate cruelty as there is for the animals that are subjected to that cruelty. Otherwise, through her judgments of others' beliefs and actions, further karma would be generated. In all her teaching, Paula exemplifies an attitude of acceptance and love, beautifully serving the needs of both her human audience and the animals in their care, without casting blame on either for the problems that occur between them. She has evolved into what is called in mythology the *wounded healer*, the one who truly understands through personal experience and who can heal from that place of understanding.

The archetype of the wounded healer is embodied by many of those people whose lives are dedicated to compassionate service. Their familiarity with the condition of those they would help may have developed through previous experiences in this lifetime or may, like Paula's, be hidden in lives other than the current one. Whatever its source, their depth of empathy and respect sets them apart, making them infinitely more effective than those who are merely sympathetic and well-intentioned. Their wound has been transformed into a gift of understanding and healing—a gift they first received themselves through suffering and then were able to share with others.

Our inner map of achieved consciousness

As we advance along the Path, we carry within us *and demonstrate* all the major stages of our development thus far, both as individuals and as a species. The biological principle *ontogeny recapitulates phylogeny** describes this process in the physical realm. All of us who have had even one class in biology will remember, for instance, that mammals manifest at an early embryonic stage the gills of their remote sea-dwelling evolutionary precursors.

This recapitulatory principle operates in terms of human *consciousness* as well as human anatomy. Present within each of us is the entire map of our unfolding of consciousness down through the ages, recapitulated emotionally and behaviorally during our development from infancy and childhood, through adolescence, to adulthood.

An example is the stage during which a great deal of the play activities of male children involve weapons—swords, guns, etc.— and mock battles to the death. Boys with no toy guns will use sticks or any available object to represent a weapon. Often par-

---

* ontogeny: the development of the individual organism
phylogeny: the evolution of a race or a genetically related group of organisms (as a species, family, or order)

ents, eager to impart nonviolent values, try to suppress what is actually a healthy expression of a normal developmental stage, a recapitulation of the evolution of physical courage in the human race. Peace-loving parents whose children relish violent games can comfort themselves with the fact that even the most altruistic adult males pass through this natural stage of childhood.

But not every child outgrows this violent stage, nor does every individual mature into someone capable of expressing humanity's highest attainments. That capacity depends on several factors: the individual's own stage of conscious evolvement, attained through the sum of completed lifetimes; the strengths and limitations of the present physical, astral/emotional, and mental bodies; and determining factors of the chosen present-life environment, including the individual's family, the overall social group, and the general culture at large. Obviously each of these factors may serve to either encourage or inhibit the fullest expression of what the individual has achieved on behalf of the soul.

In a rather unusual illustration of this, a psychic friend of mine was asked by a married couple to do a reading on their retarded daughter. Part of her reading follows.

Going deep into meditation, I merge with this child and am astonished to experience the happy, peaceful state in which she dwells. I am aware of a profound and dedicated intelligence connected with this child, one who has carried through lifetime after lifetime the heavy responsibility of imparting difficult teachings in order to raise the consciousness of others. The soul has permitted her in this lifetime to be taken care of and do little besides cheerfully exist, letting others carry the responsibilities. Hers is not a shirking of duty in this lifetime, but rather an exploration of a different kind of physical-plane experience and an alternate approach to the soul's task. For though the child is not presently accomplishing anything notable on the outer plane, she is still very much the teacher, serving as a powerful catalyst for raising consciousness in the parents who adore her.

I am told by my Guides that children such as this are not who they are and what they are in response to their own karma so much as a consequence of their parents' karma. While it is more or less a lifetime of limbo for such children, their presence has a most powerful effect on those with whom they are closely associated, bringing out surprising qualities from their depths.

When my friend gave her reading to these parents, they exclaimed that their child's sweet presence in their lives had taught them much they were sure they couldn't otherwise have learned. Obviously not every such child is experienced as a blessing to those responsible for its welfare. Indeed, often the case is quite the opposite. But each is always a catalyst for some degree of transformation, as was the child described above.

Outer appearances vs. inner development

Every incarnation presents greater or lesser degrees of challenge, always in the service of transformation. This transformative process goes on all the time but is concealed in the daily details of our lives. As we have seen, it is further obscured because we are not all moving in the same direction at the same time. Sometimes, though the outer conditions of our lives may be similar, we may actually be eons apart in development. For instance, imagine three men all incarcerated in the same prison for felony convictions.

The first, a young man of twenty-two, together with two friends assaulted a man who emerged drunk from a bar, robbed him, and beat him senseless. Alcoholism, drug addiction, and violence were a part of this young man's family life and the life of the neighborhood where he grew up. His low impulse control, lack of judgment, and capacity for reckless violence may be attributed to his chaotic childhood and to the probability that he is at an early point on the Outward Path.

The second inmate, thirty-five, well educated, and previously the vice president of a large investment firm, was convicted of an intricately plotted and expertly executed "white collar" crime, a scam that bilked millions of dollars from hapless investors. His crime was perpetrated neither on impulse nor out of need, but rather as the kind of exercise in power that appealed to him as someone approaching the Point of Integration.

The third prisoner committed an armed robbery under the influence of alcohol. This man, too, was young and from an impoverished, chaotic, and violent background. Two of his brothers were also in prison and another has already died violently.

Years later, after all three have served their sentences, this third man returns to the same prison, now as a sober member of Alcoholics Anonymous and a representative of AA's outreach to hospitals and institutions. He has a good life on the outside, with a steady job as a construction foreman and a girlfriend he plans to marry. He also has a mission to carry the message inside to other incarcerated alcoholics. His own experience as an inmate gives him credibility with the other prisoners who join him in AA meetings. His commitment to serving these men is characteristic of someone on the Path of Return. No doubt his crime and incarceration are a recapitulation of an earlier, unfinished phase in his soul's development while his area of service—in prisons and with alcoholics—is remediation for those actions from an earlier lifetime.

This greatly oversimplified example is meant to show that a person's point on the Path is not easily discerned from circumstances of birth or degrees of education or from labels such as "convicted felon." People at every stage of evolvement may be found in all walks of life and at every level of society. Further, like our imaginary third prisoner, they may be recapitulating a much-earlier phase of their development in order to eventually bring greater consciousness and the possibility of remediation to that particular realm of experience.

Finding your place on the Path

It is natural that, having read all of the above, you might wonder where you are on the Path. Are you on the Outward Path, seeking greater identification with and command of your physical body, developing physical courage and a sense of self? Are you reaching the Point of Integration, eager to flex your powers to lead, to command, to control, to influence people and events? Or are you on the Path of Return, aiming to meet and remediate your unresolved karma through understanding and service?

Because you are drawn to the material contained in this book, you are doubtless either approaching or already at the Point of Integration or you are just beginning to move off that point and onto the Path of Return. At an earlier phase of your evolution of consciousness, you would have little or no interest in the subjects covered here. At a later point on the Path of Return the material is equally irrelevant, because you will have progressed to more Universal and less personal concerns.

It is likely if you are reading this book that you are at the turning point of the hero's journey. But remember, that turning point, given the vast scale of your journey, stretches over lifetimes. I'm reminded of what a man who had spent many years at sea told me about piloting a supertanker.

"First," he said, "you discover, for whatever reasons, that you're headed for trouble. Maybe you're off course. Maybe something's up ahead that shouldn't be there and you've got to avoid it. So you throttle down the engines. Once the propellers have stopped turning, you reverse their direction to stop the ship's forward motion. You give more and more power to those reversed propellers but still, for a long time, that ship keeps right on moving at pretty much the same speed and in more or less the same direction. It takes a while, when you're dealing with that much weight and mass and momentum, before there's any outward sign that you're going to be able to change your course." Perhaps our lives at this turning point are a bit like the immense ship in the hands of its captain. To all outer appearances we are driven farther and farther from shore by the very momentum of our journey. Yet, already set in motion by the Intelligence that guides us are the forces that will bring us to a halt, turn us around, and draw us back toward home.

The purpose of uncertainty

One of our greatest challenges while in physical incarnation is that we cannot know where we're going, much less whether or not we'll get there. At this critical turning point when we are most consciously introspective, most sensitive to and troubled by our own and others' suffering, we must constantly battle not only those difficult outer conditions we face but all our inner doubts and fears as well.

Why, you may ask, must it be so difficult? The whole process would be so much more efficient if we were given our tasks and could simply set about accomplishing them in a straightforward way. Why must the mystery, the blind groping for direction be added to our burdens? Why can't we *know*?

The Moon card in tarot signifies those times when even God hides his face—our times of deepest doubt, our dark night of the soul. During such periods many of us seek the advice of psychics, astrologers, others skilled in the art of divination. Whether or not such readings are accurate and helpful depends on several factors: the psychic's skill, the level of attunement that day, the energetic rapport between our Guides and the psychic's Guides (because in a good reading whatever our Guides are able to com-

Reunion with Source

Elevation beyond physical matter

- Refined physical vehicle
- Identification with Higher Mind/Soul
- Exploration of spiritual realms/truth-seeking
- Development of group consciousness
- Action taken after meditation, deliberation
- Karma overcome through remediation and service
- Soul works through inspiration of Higher Self
- Altruistic conscience: "It's wrong if it hurts humanity"
- Higher psychic attunement through ajna center
- Universal compassion
- Motivated by desire to serve

<   <   <   <   <   <

expansion   **expansion • experience**

Test: spiritual courage

Old soul

Path of Return

Outward Path

Young soul

Test: physical courage

expression   **expression • experience**

>   >   >   >   >   >

Separation from Source

Descent into physical matter

- Coarse physical vehicle
- Identification with physical body/personality
- Exploration of physical limits/sensation-seeking
- Development of physical capacities
- Low impulse control
- Karma generated through physical acts
- Other-directed (good soldier, team member, follower)
- Primitive conscience: "It's wrong if I get caught"
- Lower psychic attunement (based in solar plexus)
- Incipient compassion
- Motivated by desire for physical gratification

The Path of Evolving Consciousness

<
<
experience

**Point of
Integration**

**Maturing soul
Test: moral
courage**

experience
>
>

- Balanced physical vehicle
- Identification with personality, intellect
- Exploration of physical power
- Development of intellect, ability to plan
- Capacity for deferred gratification
- Karma generated through use of power,
  manipulation of others
- Self-directed (good leader, influential citizen,
  celebrity)
- Developed consciousness: "It's wrong if it hurts
  those I care for"
- Psychic attunement shifting from solar plexus
  to ajna center
- Considerable compassion
- Motivated by desire for recognition and
  influence

municate to the psychic's Guides is then translated by the psychic back to us), whether the psychic's spiritual development can accommodate whatever of a spiritual nature is being communicated to us, whether we are so threatened by any portion of the reading that we distort or disregard it, and finally, whether it is yet time for us to know more, to be reassured with a promise of better things to come, or whether we must continue in the dark a while longer.

When I was thirty-five and going through the bleakest period of my adult life, I visited a psychic for the first time. She was a tarot reader and amazingly accurate. Some of her predictions began to come about almost as soon as I left her office! For many months I played the tape of our session every morning as I got ready for work because her promise that things would get better helped me hang on while Fortune's wheel slowly turned to a more beneficent position.

When at forty-two I found myself directionless after abandoning most of the goals I had pursued and achieved, I again sought the help of psychics. But now no one could read accurately for me. In desperation I taught myself astrology, palmistry, and tarot, hoping thereby to unlock the mystery I was living. These tools helped me to think symbolically, to sharpen my intuition, and to understand my children and all my significant relationships to a far deeper degree than my knowledge of psychology had made possible. I learned so much that eventually my entire view of life changed. Yet the answers I sought regarding my own situation continued to elude me.

Looking back it's clear why every door had to remain closed to me for all those years. Only thus could my despair motivate my search for understanding, while my impatience and self-will were tempered by time.

It's clear, too, why none of the psychics I consulted could do much to ease this difficult passage. To do so would have interfered with the necessary process—a little like pulling up carrots to see how they're growing.

When we seek a clearer comprehension of our soul's agenda for our present incarnation, when we want to better understand and cooperate with God's will for our life, we are exercising the *only* valid reason for either studying the occult or for consulting with those who do. But when we try to use our own or another's psychic gifts and occult powers to indulge our self-will, we are employing black magic, putting ourselves in danger of postponing rather than facilitating our enlightenment. And of course we must remember that psychics' skills and ethics vary widely, just as do those of the members of any other profession. As in every other area of our life, we need to use discernment regarding whom we consult about our fate and the future. But we must also recognize that there are times when no one, no matter how gifted, can help us to see ahead because our hopes and fears are needed. They are working on us, deepening our character and ripening our consciousness.

Imagine for a moment that you are a young man of seventeen with considerable athletic prowess that you've spent years of practice developing. Right now, tonight, you're out on the football field playing against your school's crosstown rival. It's the homecoming game and the stands above you are filled. Your parents are up there. So is your girlfriend. You've heard there might be a couple of scouts up there, too, and your coach has hinted that a scholarship could depend on how you play tonight.

The teams are well-matched and sometimes the play gets rough, but your will to win is blazing, focused to a laser point. Nothing, nothing has ever mattered as much as winning does tonight.

Now, as you imagine yourself in this picture, add one more element—that you already know the outcome of the game.

It changes everything, doesn't it?

When the anxiety attendant to not knowing the outcome is removed, *so is all your motivation.* We pay a high price in disturbed emotions because we aren't able to predict whether a given situation will turn out the way we hope or the way we fear. But knowing ahead of time exacts its own price—the flattening of our emotions as the buoyancy of hope, the thrill of anticipation, and the compelling drive of desire all are rendered irrelevant. When we already know the outcome of any challenging situation, the spur to stretch, to reach, to grow is removed. In fact, it can no longer even be termed a challenge. It is simply an event to be lived through.

Now imagine, if you will, that you are that same young man of seventeen but that, in addition to knowing the outcome of tonight's game, you also know whether or not the scholarship will materialize and all of the other details about how the life ahead of you will unfold up to and including the circumstances of your death. Your entire life is like a book you've already read. There will be no shocks but no happy surprises, either—nothing but the sequential unfolding of events over the years. . . .

Can you feel the weight of that knowing? How it would rob every joyous occasion of its effervescence, because you would know that in its sparkling footsteps will follow eventually the heavy tread of the next misfortune?

No, we must go at life blindly or not at all, because if we *knew*, we would *resist*. We would try to circumvent the painful episodes, avoid the difficult relationships, forestall the catastrophes. And we'd be resisting, preventing, circumventing, and forestalling our own evolution, brought about precisely *through* these experiences and the ways we must change in order to accommodate them.

A hero is such because he faces the unknown bravely until finally, after great effort, he prevails. Sometimes he has a magical sword or a fabulous steed to lend him an extra edge as he battles his ogres and dragons. We, too, can use all the helpful tools we can find to give us strength: prayer and meditation, a spiritual discipline, inspirational literature, a support group of peers who are dealing with problems like our own.

And we can remind ourselves that in all our struggles with life, in all our battles with our doubts and fears, even when we think we are failing miserably, our every attempt to find our way both stretches us spiritually and proves our heroism.

Eight

How Can I Help Myself and Others to Heal?

Perhaps you've heard the story of the farmer who lived in an out-of-the-way hamlet and who one day discovered his cow had gotten out of her pasture and disappeared. As he began searching for her he met his neighbor, who asked where the farmer was going. When he replied that his cow was lost, the neighbor shook his head and said, "That's bad luck."

"Good luck, bad luck. Who's to say?" replied the farmer, who went on his way. Out in the hills beyond the cultivated farmland, he found his cow grazing alongside a beautiful horse, and when he led his cow home the horse followed along behind her.

The next morning his neighbor came by to ask about the cow. Seeing her back in her pasture beside a beautiful horse, he asked the farmer what had happened. The farmer explained that the horse had followed his cow home and the neighbor explained, "That's good luck!"

"Good luck, bad luck. Who's to say?" replied the farmer, and he went on with his chores.

The following day the farmer's son returned home on leave

from the army. He immediately tried to ride the beautiful horse but was thrown to the ground and broke his leg. When the neighbor passed by on his way to market and saw the young man sitting on the porch with his leg splinted and bandaged while his father hoed the garden, the neighbor asked what had happened. When he heard, he shook his head.

"That's bad luck," he said.

"Good luck, bad luck. Who's to say?" replied the farmer, continuing to hoe his garden.

The next day the boy's unit came marching down the road. Overnight, war had broken out and they were off to battle. When the son couldn't join them, the neighbor, leaning over the fence and calling to the farmer in his field, commented that at least the father was spared losing his son in war.

"That's good luck," shouted the neighbor.

"Good luck, bad luck. Who's to say?" replied the farmer who went on plowing.

That night the farmer and his son sat down to eat their dinner, and after a few bites the son choked on a chicken bone and died. At the funeral the neighbor put his hand on the farmer's shoulder and said sadly, "That's bad luck."

"Good luck, bad luck. Who's to say?" replied the farmer, placing an armload of flowers beside the casket.

Later that week the neighbor came by to tell the farmer that his son's entire unit had been massacred.

"At least you were with your son when he died. That's good luck," said the neighbor.

"Good luck, bad luck. Who's to say?" replied the farmer, and he went on his way to market.

And so on . . .

———

Most of us are like the neighbor in this little tale. Every reaction and judgment we have is based on what is occurring at a given point in our unfolding story. Is a particular event a blessing or is it a curse? We let our emotions decide. But if somehow we were magically freed of emotion—especially fear whenever adversity strikes—then we wouldn't call it adversity at all. We would simply call it "change," because that is what every unforeseen event or condition requires of us—that to some degree we change.

Adversity defined as the fear of change

The two concepts, adversity and change, are so inextricably linked that we tend to measure the severity of any difficulty by the degree of change it demands. We define ourselves through the conditions and circumstances we experience daily, and we resist their alteration out of a very basic fear of loss of our identity. Who will we be if we can no longer do what we are used to doing in the same, habitual way? Will we be able to cope, to meet the challenge? We know, instinctively, that too much change, too much stress, more than we can adapt to, undermines both our physical and mental health. It *devitalizes* us.

And yet change is necessary to all life, is in fact the very essence of livingness. When it is blocked, there is a lack of flow of vital energy, resulting in either the torpor of stagnation or the frozen rigidity of crystallization. Adversity, because it *forces* us to change, stirs us up, shakes us out of old habits, stretches us, demands that unused parts of us awaken and develop. It *revitalizes* us.

So which is it, revitalizing or devitalizing? Energizing or debilitating? Change can be either. And it can be both.

There is a card in tarot called the Tower, depicting the sudden explosive force of catastrophe. It depicts a tower blasted in two by a great bolt of lightning and two helpless human figures hurtling headfirst toward the earth. This is obviously a card signifying sudden calamity, disaster, an emergency—all the eventualities we most dread. No one is happy to see the Tower appear in a tarot spread. But the Tower is sometimes necessary because it also indicates the breaking up of hard conditions, the end of stagnation, *a sudden event that releases frozen energy.* Any emergency calls forth, indeed demands our highest and most heroic human qualities and capabilities. The best that is in us is required to *emerge.* People often report that while facing the demand for action under the duress of an emergency, they felt most alive, most in touch with their innate power and beingness, most connected with all of Life. They were swept above and beyond their day-to-day identity—that very identity to which all of us normally cling most tenaciously. In the face of great danger, the ever-present veneer was dropped, caution abandoned, and heretofore untapped capacities for leadership and decisive action emerged in a heroic moment of integration, honesty, and truth. Such moments, when well realized in a film or play, move us to applaud or to cry because we recognize that the character involved is now forever altered, ineffably and mysteriously expanded, more truly him- or herself than before.

The major events that bring about changes in our own lives are rarely of a moment's duration, but even if they are brief and cataclysmic, their effects work out over weeks, months, years, decades. And unlike the stoic farmer of the story, we react, we adapt, we alter our definition of ourselves.

Catastrophic change and healing

In a given incarnation we may be poised on the brink of healing a condition that has been present for many lifetimes. As the following story demonstrates, traumatic experiences and cata-strophic changes may provide the necessary catalyst for deep healing.

Barbara, in her forties, radiates quiet strength in spite of a pronounced limp and a withered arm. There are soft laugh lines around her eyes, as well as lines etched by the constant physical pain she endures—and other subtler lines, too, that hint at a personal knowledge of the Tower's lightning blast. Here in her own words is Barbara's story:

My sister Paige and I look nothing alike, but we were so close in age, only seven months apart, that when we were little our parents were constantly asked if we were twins.

I used to cringe every time I heard them answer. They'd say, "Well, you see, Barbara's adopted," but it was worse when I was old enough to answer the question myself. There was something about having to say "It's because I'm ad-opted" that made me feel as though I'd been born on the moon, especially because whoever asked would then look from my blond, blue-eyed parents and sister to me, with my hazel eyes, olive skin, and dark brown hair (I am half-Hispanic by birth) and say, "Oh. Well, then, *that* explains it."

To me it seemed that the fact that I was adopted certainly did explain a lot! My parents finally got exactly what they wanted when Paige was born, and somehow I had been the lucky charm (I heard *that* countless times, too) that brought about her birth. Somehow I got the credit for Perry, too, our baby brother, who came along two years after Paige. To put it bluntly, I grew up feeling like a cross between a rabbit's foot, a mongrel dog from the pound, and a visitor from outer space—never really part of the family.

I've often wondered if that constant emphasis on my being adopted, along with the fact that I looked so different, too, had something to do with what happened between me and our grandfather. Twice a week, starting when Paige and I were eight and Perry was six, our grandfather would pick us all up from school to take them to horseback riding lessons. I was allergic to horses, so he would deliver them to the barn and then take me to his house for a couple of hours until it was time to pick them up and bring us all home.

While I was at his house, we played games together. Grandpa was a widower, so we were always alone. The games got a little complicated and gradually became sexual, but I was too young to really understand what he was doing to me. Basically I was molested during those afternoons for nearly three years.

There was a trick I found out I could do. I could leave my body, take my consciousness elsewhere while my grandfather was doing what he did. I'd go up to the ceiling, out the window, sometimes to places that were pretty unearthly. I realize now it was the only way I could protect myself. Even if he was doing those things to my body, he wasn't really doing them to *me*. I was somewhere else.

I could never tell anyone what was going on. I don't think I felt I had any right to be protected. So it didn't end until I went to junior high school, got involved in after-school sports, and took the bus home. Coincidentally, my grandfather started playing cards in the afternoon and told Mom he couldn't drive Paige and Perry anymore.

Anyway, like most people who go through something like this, I put all those memories in a deep, dark place, covered them over without a trace, and went on with my life which, for other reasons, wasn't too easy. I was a good student but socially I just couldn't find a niche. We lived in a small town on the coast of central California during the fifties, when there were still lots of farms and orchards. Mexican laborers worked for white landowners, and the economic and social classes were drawn basically along racial lines. Because of my adoptive family, I was definitely too Anglo and too middle class to hang out with the Hispanics, yet I was a little too Latin to really fit in with the mostly blond, blue-eyed friends of my sister and brother. At least I was good at tennis. That kept me busy and gave me an identity of sorts.

I finally left home for college. Once I was off on my own, I started supporting myself and I never looked back. I graduated with a degree in physical education and got a wonderful job teaching tennis in a high school. I loved my work so much, maybe because it was still only as an athlete that I felt like a real person.

Then one rainy Sunday evening that whole life ended. I

was driving home with my groceries when another car broadsided me at forty-five miles an hour.

By the time the ambulance arrived at the hospital I was pretty much gone. The paramedics told me later they thought they'd lost me. Some minutes went by with no vital signs, but they didn't give up and finally I came around.

Or maybe it would be more accurate to say I came *back*. Because I had definitely been somewhere other than here.

I was in the hospital for a long time, and one of the interns who was interested in near-death experiences—NDEs—came to talk to me a few times. She knew I'd been clinically dead for several minutes and tried to get me to tell her about whatever I remembered from that time. Actually I remembered everything, but I wasn't willing to talk about it for quite a while. It was too special, too personal, too *big* for me to talk about with anyone. Even putting it into words reduced it somehow, and I wanted to hang onto exactly the way it had been.

Even today I really can't find words to describe it accurately. I try but it still comes out so flat. First there was a roaring noise and I was speeding through a tunnel, the way it might feel to be sucked into a huge vacuum-cleaner hose. Then everything opened up into this incredibly beautiful light that wasn't only around me but within me as well, suffusing me with the greatest warmth and peace. It was so soft, so comforting and healing.

I found myself in the presence of a Being from whom I felt the most complete acceptance and love I have ever known and with whom I watched all the prior events of my life unfold as though I were watching a film. I had this tremendous clarity about every detail of my life and how necessary all of it, even the worst parts, had been. And then I was lovingly persuaded by this Being, who knew me utterly and accepted me completely, to return here.

The entire experience was one of incredible objectivity. I know that doesn't seem to fit with what we usually think of as love, but that's what it was. I saw *everything* that had happened to me throughout my life with the deepest love and understanding.

When I came back to life in this body, nothing seemed very important except bringing back with me as much of that love and light and *knowing* as I possibly could.

To say the experience changed my life would be the greatest understatement. For one thing my career and my identity as an athlete were utterly wiped out the moment the other car hit me. I'm not going to dwell on my physical recovery. It's enough to say that it was long and difficult and painful. But maybe all those months spent convalescing forced me to hold still long enough to really take in what had happened to me on a nonphysical level. It was as though the old me with all her negativity and fears, all her sorrow and shame and self-pity and bitterness, was given a brand-new perspective on her past. And this new perspective included a level of love and understanding that just wiped out all that negativity. Not the memories, just all the bad feelings connected with them, so that they were healed. In fact, everything I once would have considered tragic now seemed perfect. I know it sounds incredible, but that's what happened.

That intern in the hospital brought me Kenneth Ring's

book *Heading toward Omega,* which describes his studies of near-death experiences. I was glad I had the book. It comforted me to know that I wasn't crazy, that I hadn't imagined the most profound experience of my life.

Not long after I got out of rehab, Dr. Ring came to town to give a lecture. Of course I went to hear him. He was doing further research to determine which people, of all those who are clinically dead for a time and then revive, actually remember their experience. It seems those who remember their NDE have often been abused in some way when they were growing up. Listening to Dr. Ring I realized that the worst part of my childhood had actually made it possible for me to bring back some of the indescribable peace and beauty of that other place. We who were abused learned, out of necessity, how to consciously leave our body and then come back again, as though we were practicing just so we could remember, later on after our NDE occurred, what it was like on the other side!

Today I use what I experienced during my NDE in my new work. I am a counselor at a hospice, and in my work with the terminally ill I share, when it is appropriate, what it's like on the other side—the healing love that awaits us when it's time to leave the physical body behind. I'm part of a team that educates members of the medical profession, the terminally ill and their family members, and anyone else who is interested regarding the subject of death and dying.

Sometimes people wonder why I'm "wasting my life" spending so much time around death. They think it must be depressing. But for me it's not depressing at all. Oh, it can be very hard work, watching someone struggle to get free of the physical body and reach that other side. But when they've done what they came to do, accomplished their purpose, and burned off whatever karma is keeping them here, it's more appropriate to regard their leave-taking as a vacation from school than a tragic event. That may sound flippant, but from my experience that's how I see it.

So when it's time for them to go on, I talk to them— sometimes when they're awake and sometimes, because it's easier, when they're sleeping. I tell them what I saw and felt and learned on the other side, what I *know* about crossing over. I'm very certain that it helps them, and today I believe it's why, after I got to the other side, I had to come back. I think this is a job I'm supposed to be doing, helping people to understand that dying isn't an end of life. It's a graduation.

Healing on the mental level

This story exemplifies many of the points delineated in this book. Barbara chose to incarnate into a family and social setting in which she felt alien, extraneous, and subtly deficient. The sexual exploitation she endured from her adoptive grandfather deepened her sense of isolation and increased her character flaw, her self-pity.

Barbara hid her vulnerability within the rigidly disciplined persona of the dedicated athlete, a role that comfortably structured her interactions with others. In adulthood she added the role of instructor to that of competitor. Only within these narrow confines could she feel safe and worthy.

Barbara's healing during her NDE was largely on the lower mental level of her energy field, the level of thoughts tinged with emotion and desire. Our distorted views about who we are, as well as the ways we are dishonest with ourselves and therefore alienated from our soul, exist on this level. Barbara's self-pity and view of herself as a victim were her principle distortions, undoubtedly generated in other incarnations, repeatedly attracting further incidents of victimization and fuel for self-pity in lifetime after lifetime. The key to healing these distortions was her achievement of *objective understanding,* brought about through contact with her soul during her NDE.

Objective understanding, the level of thought untinged with emotion or desire, is of the higher mental level, the level whereon the soul dwells. It is our own soul which we encounter when we leave the physical body and experience the postmortem review. Barbara's contact with her soul healed her distorted beliefs, bringing about a healing of her distorted emotional field as well. Any correction on the higher levels of the human energy field promotes, through induction, corresponding corrections on the lower levels of the field. It was at her soul's behest that she returned to the Earth plane and continued her work here in this lifetime.

And as Barbara so correctly surmised, her ability to leave her body, developed in order to cope with the repeated molestations she suffered as a child, was the key to retaining the memory of her healing.

What if Barbara had been somehow saved from her history of early sexual abuse? Would she then have had to forego as well her conscious memory of the transcendent beauty of her NDE, with all of its transformative influence?

It is difficult for us to remember, in the face of emotionally charged issues such as sexual abuse, that dwelling within every tragedy, every trauma, every occasion of adversity are the precious seeds of healing—healing not only for that event or condition but healing for much that cannot be seen or even intuited. Perhaps it is not overstatement to say that saving Barbara from her awful childhood crucifixion would have prevented in adulthood her precious transfiguration.

And so what then *is* healing?

The nature of healing

True healing occurs at levels far more subtle than the physical and involves energetic configurations that have persisted throughout many lifetimes. Freeing the emotional body from the distortions and illusions within it has a highly beneficial effect on physical functioning, but the most profound healing possible is that of our mental bodies.

Everything we are while incarnate emanates from the mental levels, for truly "as a man thinketh, so is he." As we proceed on the Outward Path from innocence to maturity, our traumas lead us to develop definite beliefs about ourselves and the nature of Life. As we begin to tread the Path of Return, our lifetimes are directed toward shedding these distortions. Imagine Barbara's higher Self, prior to this lifetime, agreeing to participate in an incarnation in which her deeply held convictions regarding her alienation and victimization were powerfully challenged. Naturally she would have to once again attract to herself, through the principle of morphogenetic resonance, those persons and events that fit with her belief system. But this time she invited the cata-lytic, cataclysmic event that made a breakthrough possible. She *asked* to be dealt the Tower card.

Remember what Barbara underwent in order to recall and be transformed by her NDE. First, the veil between consciousness in the physical state and consciousness while in the nonphysical was thinned as she learned to leave her body while being mo-lested. Then she was injured so badly that she was forced out of her physical body. Finally, although she ultimately recovered, some of the crippling effects of her physical trauma remained. This was the price, agreed upon prior to her present incarnation, for the enlightenment she gained, the profound healing she underwent.

Guidelines for healing ourselves

Inevitably, even those of us who are deeply committed to our spiritual evolution, struggle against adversity. We need the help of guidelines to remind us how to cooperate with our transforma-tional process.

A list of such guidelines is offered here.

- Always look for the gift in adversity
- Never indulge in self-pity
- Never blame anyone else for your problems
- Cultivate an attitude of gratitude
- Do not judge your condition or that of others
- Avoid sentimentality
- Recognize that disease is not a punishment

- Seek opportunities to serve
- Learn to regard death as a healing

Now let us take a closer look at each of these guidelines.

Always look for the gift in adversity

Every problem is an assignment from your soul. Therefore, acknowledge that a purpose is being served by your problem, your wound, your illness, your disability, your terminal condition, and try to align with it; that is, seek what it is trying to teach you. Remember that from the soul's perspective, a change in consciousness is of far greater value than a "cure." Therefore, follow King Solomon's wise injunction: "With all your getting, get understanding." Make that understanding the object of your quest and be optimistic that you will be rewarded.

There is a delightful story about two small boys, one an optimist and the other a pessimist. The pessimist is led to a room filled with all kinds of wonderful toys, but as soon as he is inside, he sits down by the door and pouts. A while later as he is led from the room, he is asked why he was so unhappy in there.

"I just *knew*," he replies miserably, "that if I chose a toy I really liked, it would probably break!"

Meanwhile the little optimist has been left in a room piled high with horse manure, where he is singing a song about cowboys and happily digging away. When invited to come out he shakes his head and keeps on digging.

"I just *know*," he calls out excitedly, "that with all this manure there's got to be a pony in here somewhere!"

Believe in the pony. Believe in the gift hidden in all the . . . well, you know. . . .

Never indulge in self-pity

You may feel that some self-pity is natural and excusable, given all that you're suffering. It is, however, an invidious indulgence that easily becomes habitual. Once the habit of self-pity is in place, it acts on our consciousness much like a drug to which we are addicted, providing a seductive excuse for further indulgence—and like the habitual use of drugs, indulgence in self-pity is an extremely effective barrier to spiritual development.

Never blame anyone else for your problems

Blaming others, like self-pity, is a self-indulgent practice that prevents us from taking responsibility for our lives. Nowhere in spiritual law is it written that someone else is to blame for our troubles, whether in this life or past lives. If we remember that all our difficulties, including those connected with other people, serve an important purpose in our evolution, then we will recognize our enemies as agents for our enlightenment. This does not mean, however, that we must necessarily enjoy all our dealings with these agents of karma.

A wise old saying advises us:

> When confronted by a foe
> Praise him,
> Bless him,
> Let him go.

Blessing our enemies, wishing them all the good we would wish for ourselves, is an excellent way to achieve our own liberation.

I once had to work in a treatment center with another therapist who repeatedly badgered and belittled me and undermined my work with our patients. From his maneuvering I learned to be more forcefully direct, and I tried to be grateful for that, but the constant struggle with him was wearing me down. I began silently affirming, "This man's highest good, whatever it is, is coming to him." One day, after I had been repeating this affirmation for a few weeks, he suddenly announced that he had been offered a far better job elsewhere and was leaving!

Such affirmations, when done with as much love as possible, put into motion the biblical injunction: "Resist ye not evil but overcome evil with good."

The higher truth behind our troubles with others is that we are really here to help one another progress along the Way. Without denying that there are problems, we can, by sending blessings, do much to ameliorate interpersonal difficulties.

Cultivate an attitude of gratitude

Sometimes when things are very dark, a review of our blessings can serve as an excellent antidote to creeping depression and self-pity. The more we focus on our blessings, the lighter our burdens become. And if we can also appreciate the progress we've already made—the lessons we've learned and the understanding we've achieved through facing previous challenges—this helps reassure us that our present difficulties will eventually yield their welcome harvest, too.

An "attitude of gratitude" isn't simply a Pollyanna attempt to gloss over or deny very real adversity. It is, rather, a spiritual discipline that involves raising our conscious focus from the negative to all the positive aspects of our condition. By gently but firmly steering our thoughts away from the negative, the positive becomes a greater part of our experienced reality.

A client who was a recovering drug addict once said to me, "Attitude is the biggest drug of all!" I would agree. And since we can choose what our attitude will be, why not choose an "upper" rather than a "downer"?

Do not judge your condition or that of others

It is virtually impossible to assess, while incarnate, where you are on the Path, nor is it usually possible until you have completed your karmic assignment to even identify whatever it is you've been learning. Although it is important to seek understanding by opening to it, a judgmental attitude regarding your progress is both inappropriate and damaging. Trust that whatever the outer conditions of your life, you *are* making progress.

Avoid comparisons with others. In the mental health program called Recovery, Incorporated, they say, "Comparisons are odious." And so they are. We are always comparing the incomparable when we judge our condition in terms of another's, because we cannot possibly see our entire picture clearly, much less someone else's.

Honor the themes being explored by your family and your group, as well as the part each of you plays, keeping in mind that we need contrast in order to learn on this plane. Sometimes that contrast comes through conflict, and therefore, someone must be the foil.

Grant each person's journey the dignity it deserves, and remember to do the same for your own. Esoterically we who incarnate here on Earth are known as "the Lords of Unceasing Devotion," an appellation that acknowledges the courage and endurance required as we travel the Path on this difficult plane. Trust that in just being here, we are all noble.

Avoid sentimentality

As we evolve spiritually, we learn to discipline our emotions, cultivate detachment, and broaden our perspective beyond what is obvious, immediate, and personal. Sentimentality is an indulgence in unenlightened emotionalism and mitigates against this kind of development by trapping us in the culture's stereotypical responses to various events. Take winning the lottery, for example. The sentimental attitude is that this is a dream come true promising untold happiness and freedom. But with the greater freedom conferred by instant millions comes greater responsibility for each choice, each action. The winner's every excuse for not being happy and fulfilled because of financial constraints is suddenly removed. The sweet hope of being happy someday is replaced by the demand to be joyous, even delirious, *now*. The number of such winners who suffer breakdowns or commit suicide indicates that contrary to popular belief, instant wealth is far from being a guarantee of bliss.

If you can appreciate that suddenly gaining the opportunity to have every material thing you've ever wanted is as great a spiritual test as losing everything you've ever loved, your viewpoint is definitely evolving.

Recognize that disease is not a punishment

Illness is not proof that we are flawed, nor does it indicate that we are not thinking positively enough. Although sometimes physical problems signal that an emotional area of life is demanding our attention, that is by no means always the case. Sometimes we suffer physically because in some mysterious way we are working through karma. According to Edgar Cayce's readings, many of those who consulted him had conditions that seemed to fit this category, illness or physical defects that were fated for that particular lifetime, chosen by the higher Self to ameliorate karma generated in an earlier lifetime.

Some illnesses are simply a condition of being in physical manifestation. We are literally made of recycled material, and there is much on the Earth plane that is energetically tainted. The Tibetan, who dictated the many volumes written by Alice Bailey, states that the purpose of all suffering is to cleanse and purify us. Therefore, whatever is the root cause of our trouble—personal problems we are ignoring or denying, karmic debts we are paying, or planetary taints we carry in our physical vehicle—we are to some degree uplifted through enduring any and every illness from which we suffer.

Seek opportunities to serve

Several of the stories in this book describe people who, having suffered themselves, become committed to helping others similarly afflicted. Such a commitment is frequently a result of greater awareness. But obviously not all of us can provide counseling, therapy, social work, etc., to others, nor should we. There are many other ways to serve. One such way is by simply continuing whatever activities we normally pursue but engaging in them with a more highly developed consciousness. The world badly needs enlightened people in every walk of life.

Some of us, due to illness or disability or other factors, are prevented from actively participating in the outer world. If this is your condition, you are nevertheless able to offer the highest kind of service of all. Thomas Merton refers to the necessary still point at the center of the wheel as the hub of the world where God can be found. If your condition forces you to hold still, then focus your awareness on whatever, whoever God is for you—and surrender to that. Become that focused point of consciousness in the center of activity.

Nothing is more effective for bringing about greater good in the world than pure thought untainted by desire. By dedicating yourself to achieving conscious contact with your Higher Power, you become a channel for those higher energies that uplift, inspire, and guide us all. Like a single mountaintop tower radioing a message of love and hope, you are, all alone and in silence, nevertheless doing enormously important spiritual work on behalf of all the rest of us who toil in the outer world.

Learn to regard death as a healing

Death is the point at which all that has been gained in a given lifetime is harvested. Often those who consult astrologers expect to be told that a loved one was under difficult aspects at the time of death. Such is not usually the case. More often the difficult aspects at the time of death appear in the survivors' charts, for it is they who must cope with both their loss and the changes it forces upon them. The person who died was often under soft, benign aspects when death came, indicating that the transition out of the body is not so much a traumatic event as an easing into another realm.

Even early, sudden, or brutal death can legitimately be regarded as a healing in that the incarnating being is released from what is, at best, the difficult task of living on the Earth plane. Esoterically, suicide and murder are regarded as wrong because they prematurely halt an individual's unfolding karmic episode, not because the life is extinguished. Life is never extinguished, never lost through what we call death.

A very wise old friend of mine who has just celebrated his hundredth birthday said to me recently about a news broadcast he'd just heard, "They say seventy-three people lost their lives today in a plane crash. Don't they know we can't lose our lives? We can only lose our bodies! They should say, 'Seventy-three people lost their *bodies* today.'"

Guidelines for helping others to heal

While many of you who read this book are seeking to heal yourselves, some of you are deeply committed to being agents of healing for others. Perhaps you've discovered that you are far more able to bear your own suffering than to watch the agony of someone close to you. In the face of another's difficulties, we all need

supportive guidelines to help us avoid sentimentality while culti-
vating detachment. Detachment is not cool indifference. Rather,
to be detached is to be *free from need* concerning the person and
the situation. When we are able to conquer our own (selfish) need
for relief from our *own* discomfort with the other person's condition, we can then offer *love* to the one in travail. And love, as
Barbara discerned during her NDE, is not a sentiment or an
emotion but a profound level of understanding and acceptance.
Nothing better promotes true healing than an atmosphere of this
very high level of love.

So, for all of us who would achieve the necessary detachment
and become agents of healing, here are a few basic guidelines. If
we would serve most effectively as healers, we must:

- Be free of need
- Recognize that we are only agents for healing, not its
  Source
- Resist being glamoured by the work and our ability to
  do it
- Be "spiritually naked" with the person we are trying
  to help
- Recognize that there may be family, group, racial, and
  planetary karmas operating
- Accept that people unconsciously *know* the reason for
  their condition
- Honor the time transformation takes

Let's now examine each of these points in more detail.

Be free of need

We must have no investment in the sufferer's recovery, in our ability to relieve suffering, or in our identity as a healer. All of these are selfish needs that interfere with our ability to be present to the sufferer and to do, with the love that comes from detachment, all that we can on behalf of that person.

Recognize that we are only agents for healing,
not its Source

Paradoxically, the less investment we have in "being a healer," the more effective an agent we become. All healing comes from the Divine. We cannot know what kind of a healing people really need, whether they need a "cure" or support as they make their transition out of the physical body. The more open we are to guidance, the better we can serve their true need.

Resist being glamoured by the work and our
ability to do it

The minister/metaphysician Catherine Ponder says, "Work is love made visible." Every kind of work, when performed with love, is a high calling. A person who is dedicated to healing with love is no more naturally exalted than another who is dedicated to performing any other kind of work with love.

Be "spiritually naked" with the person we are trying to help

Do not hide in falsely cheerful clichés, subterfuge, or indifference and impersonality. Watching another's suffering tests our faith, and we must allow ourselves to care without needing a specific response or outcome. We must honor the ways in which we ourselves are changed by participating in another's suffering, dying, or physical recovery.

Recognize that there may be family, group, racial, and planetary karmas operating

To some degree these karmas are always operating, submerging personal destiny within a larger context with wider implications. By playing a part in the unfolding of these greater karmas, every individual life serves to advance the entire group.

Accept that people unconsciously know the reason for their condition and will resist "losing it" until it has served its transformative purpose

When we attempt to save another from an illness or problem, we may inadvertently be interfering with that person's reason for incarnation—the enlightenment he or she is pursuing under the direction of the soul. This is especially challenging when the person we want to help is our child. Honor another's path, another's karma. If watching is too painful, we need to get help for *ourselves* to better handle our own suffering.

Honor the time transformation takes

Because we dwell in the plane of dense physical matter, true change happens slowly. Even when an effect seems to be brought about suddenly, the individual's preparation for it may have taken lifetimes.

One final suggestion that applies whether we hope to be healed or to heal another: trust that we are evolving.

In other words, have faith. Pay less attention to the evening news and more attention to how greatly global consciousness has been raised just in the last fifty years. Think of some of the concepts that were radical a few decades ago—e.g., minority rights, women's rights, protection of the environment. These are an accepted part of our shared cultural value system today. Things *are* changing for the better—globally, internationally, culturally, and personally. If you step back and achieve some perspective, you can see the changes and feel them working on all of us.

Healing and enlightenment

Perhaps by now, having read so much about the healing effects of suffering, you are asking, "But what about healing through joy?" Certainly all of us but the most masochistic would choose, if we could, that our enlightenment come about through joyous expansions of consciousness rather than by adversity's grim lessons. Why then, does the balance of our experience often seem more heavily weighted with the grievous than with the rapturous? This is because we tend to *remember* our times of affliction longer and with greater clarity than we do our times of ecstasy. Then, too, they last longer. Compare those light, fleeting, evanescent moments of joy you've known with sorrow's seemingly everlasting pall. In the symbology of astrology, the planet Saturn, also known as the Greater Malefic, is the teacher that forces us to learn our hard lessons. Saturn is also linked with Cronus, or Father Time. Because teaching—and learning—take time, tribulation is a better teacher than delight.

Still, joy and suffering are not so much opposites as states that exist in spiraling counterpoint to each other—anguish leading to understanding, understanding leading to joy, joy healing the effects of the anguish that eventually brought about the understanding, and so on. If we were to separate the spiral into pieces, we might say that enlightenment comes through adversity, while healing comes through joy. In fact, they are joined in an overall process that allows us to both rebalance and advance.

You have been gradually introduced in this book to a redefinition of healing, one that is not necessarily tied to the reduction or cure of physical or psychological distress. Rather, healing is redefined herein as a vast process that overrides the boundaries of life and death and makes use of every experience to advance understanding and every occasion of adversity to restore balance. Further, from the perspective presented herein, each evolving human being is viewed as a tiny but significant and necessary part of the entire body of humanity, which is itself an evolving entity. This wider evolution is brought about as each of us contributes our increasing capacity to hold light.

In human beings this capacity is increased by our greater understanding or consciousness, our enlightenment. As we achieve greater consciousness, each of our energy bodies—the physical/etheric, the emotional or astral, and the lower mental and higher mental—all glow more brightly. This increased radiance occurs because higher thought brings about a refinement of all grades of matter, whether dense or subtle, creating more space between particles. This space between particles is filled with light.

All evolution involves the capacity to hold light. The evolution of dense physical-plane matter is one of the tasks of incarnating human beings. We effect this evolution as our growing consciousness brings about the refinement of the cellular, molecular, and atomic material of our dense physical vehicle. As we achieve greater rapport with our soul, we serve as an increasingly conscious part of the bridge our soul forms between the dense physical matter which we inhabit and Spirit. This Spirit is our Source, as well as the Source of all manifestation.

Esoterically it might be stated that *what is actually being healed by all human beings incarnate is the restriction or limitation of consciousness imposed when that consciousness must express through dense physical matter.* Just as higher-capacity electrical transformers are necessary if greater power loads are to be tolerated and transmitted, so must we expand physical matter's capacity to hold and transmit more and more of the available Universal light. One of our jobs here on Earth is to bring greater consciousness to physical matter, to redeem it, if you will.

Therefore each time you undergo some trauma, adversity, or tragedy, or observe another doing so, ask yourself "Will this experience *ultimately* contribute to deeper understanding and therefore greater enlightenment?"

If you ask from a wide enough perspective and with great
enough detachment, your answer will always be yes.

Yes to Life.

Yes to this life of yours.

Yes to your struggles and disappointments and challenges.

Yes to your lessons and opportunities and victories.

Yes to your growing, glowing radiance.

Yes.

Afterword

I t is a new millennium—and the end of a two-thousand-year-long Age as well. As we moved out of the twentieth century and into the twenty-first, and out of the Piscean Age into the Age of Aquarius, powerful forces for change began working on each of us individually, on the body of humanity as a whole, and on the entire planet as well. Increasingly during these decades of transition, we are seeing the barriers between individuals, societies, races, and nations being bridged, breaking down, or dissolving. Three global realities are among the many forces working to bring about the dissolution of these barriers.

First of all is overpopulation with all its attendant consequences, among which are vanishing wilderness and wildlife, increasing urbanization, diminishing natural resources, environmental pollution, and global warming. Today we are presented with critical issues only a *worldwide* consensus can address. Anything less cannot effect the necessary changes to save us and our planet.

Second, instant worldwide communication is shrinking the

distances both literally and figuratively between us and our brothers and sisters all over the globe. How far apart can East and
West, or the northern and southern hemispheres, really be when
we all see the same television broadcasts, follow the same fashion
trends, know immediately of each other's national news and crises?

The third major factor is the threat to continuing life on this
planet posed by modern military technology. Even though con-
flicting interests continue to divide nations, our shared fate as
casualties of any global confrontation unites us in our hope for
personal survival.

If our regard for one another's welfare is at first largely self-
serving, motivated by such concerns as "I won't make it if the
planet doesn't" or "Without economic aid that country may
threaten mine with nuclear blackmail," nevertheless progress
is being made. As outer pressures continue to encourage the
development of positive inner qualities, a genuinely selfless
consideration will, in time, develop. This outer pressure on inner
consciousness is how spiritual evolution works through every Age.

An Age is a cycle of approximately two thousand years, and
during each such cycle a vast theme is developed within the consciousness of humanity—a theme related to the astrological sign
governing the cycle and for which the age is named. *Group consciousness* is the theme for the Aquarian Age, and the simple
statement "We are all in this together" concisely expresses the
lesson ahead for humanity, a lesson necessary for our spiritual
evolution and our physical survival as well.

We have now entered the Aquarian Age. The sign of Aquarius
is connected with the social order, with friends, groups, and as we
have seen, with group consciousness. Most of us were first made
aware of the "dawning of the Age of Aquarius" when we heard

the lyrics from the sixties musical *Hair*. Since then the term *New Age* has become commonplace in spite of not yet being widely understood.

It is difficult to say exactly when the New Age or the Age of Aquarius begins, because zodiacal signs in the heavens do not have precise boundaries. An Age is defined by the astrological sign in which the polestar appears at the time of equinox. For a period of approximately two thousand years the polestar appears in a given sign and acts as a transmitter to Earth for the particular energetic emanations produced by that linked group of stars. We move from one Age to the next as the polestar slowly transits out of one sign of the zodiac and into another. Some astrologers claim the New Age began as early as the 1850s. Others say it won't start until well into the twenty-first century. Many accept the year 2000 as the approximate turning point, and *all* agree that we are definitely in the throes of the transition right now.

The Piscean Age, also known as the Age of Faith, is ending. Throughout much of the world for most of these last two thousand years, organized religion has held a position of importance in the individual's life nearly inconceivable to many of us today. The goal of this Age has been personal transformation or salvation through devotion to a distant deity—primarily to Buddha in the East and to Jesus Christ in the West. Both these great Beings embodied and taught the global lesson of the Age—*compassion*. We are exhorted to love our enemies as well as our friends by a Savior who prayed for forgiveness of his enemies even as they crucified him. The cynical adage "Jesus gave us pity: the Greeks gave us everything else" at least acknowledges that he did indeed impart this lesson well. Pity, kindliness, and patience were repeatedly emphasized by the Buddha as the cornerstones for all his teachings regarding living correctly and finding salvation through freedom from reincarnation.

If the last two thousand years of wars, barbarism, religious persecution and genocide, including the recent horrors of the Holocaust and Vietnam, indicate that we still have a long way to go in learning this lesson of compassion, remember this: today great numbers of people naturally and automatically demonstrate the same quality of compassion that was at one time a radical and nearly incomprehensible ideal. Today we are shocked not by the presence of compassion but by its absence. Most of us at least acknowledge one another's pain and suffering, and many persons are moved to make enormous personal sacrifices in order to ameliorate the suffering of others with whom they may have little in common besides their shared humanity. Though not all of us have learned this lesson of compassion, many of us have learned it well. The Tibetan predicted that at the end of the Piscean Age, the expression of compassion would even be overdone. Isn't overdoing compassion—doing for others what they could do for themselves—the chief trait of many co-alcoholics and other codependents who find themselves in a significant relationship with an addicted person? Isn't this a widespread flaw among many parents today, as well as many members of the helping professions? Now some of us are having to learn to temper our overdeveloped compassion with the equally spiritual Aquarian traits of detachment and impersonality, learning to honor each individual's responsibility for his or her place on the Path.

Just as the Piscean Age has also been called the Age of Faith, so the Aquarian Age is also known as the Age of Man—not for the male gender but because this will be an Age that sees the flowering of humanity's capacity for creation. As we achieve greater control over our emotional and mental faculties and learn to work in spiritual concert together, we will consciously create the emotional and mental realms we inhabit, just as today we build our physical environment.

All the Aquarian emphasis on group consciousness is balanced somewhat through the energetic influence of Leo, the sign brought into prominence now due to its opposition to Aquarius. Leo urges independence and individuality, personal responsibility for every action. Together these two opposites, Aquarius and Leo, guide us toward deepened sensitivity to the welfare of the group while demanding that we stand as individuals on our own two feet. What a powerful and hopeful direction for humanity in the coming Age!

On this steadily shrinking planet each of us is now, as never before, our brother's keeper. For the first time, great numbers of us throughout the world are psychologically astute, aware of our own feelings, behaviors, and motivations and those of others. At the same time we are becoming more psychically attuned to one another and to other dimensions of existence. The time is coming when there can no longer be the present isolation and insulation regarding "my loss" or "your need," "his pain" or "her hunger." Increasingly we will feel one another's burdens and hopefully become willing to help bear them, recognizing them to be our own as well. The beautiful teachings of the Piscean Age—love, sensitivity, compassion, and forgiveness—will stand us in good stead as we learn to extend them not only to our brother and sister close at hand but to everyone everywhere, to the entire body of humanity, of which we are a part.

Recommended Reading

Bailey, Alice. *Initiation, Human and Solar*. Lucis Publishing Company, New York, 1922.

This is Bailey's first work. If it appeals to you, then you will probably want to read her other books as well.

Brennan, Barbara Ann. *Hands of Light: A Guide to Healing Through the Human Energy Field*. Bantam Books, New York, 1987.

The definitive work on hands-on healing, this book contains very fine illustrations of the chakras, the subtle bodies, and the energetic configurations of health and disease.

de Hartog, Jan. *The Spiral Road*. Harper & Row, New York, 1957.

My favorite work of fiction, de Hartog's book is a compelling study of the roles good and evil play as we tread the Path toward enlightenment. It is, as well, an evocative examination of the spiral nature of all evolution.

Karagulla, Sharafica. *Breakthrough to Creativity: Your Higher Sense Perception*. De Vorss, Los Angeles, 1967.

Written by a medical doctor, this is a book about integrating high sense perception and energetic healing with traditional medical approaches to disease. The author writes with deep respect both for the scientific methods in which she was trained and for the subtler dimensions of reality that so powerfully affect our physical state.

Kunz, Dora van Gelder. *The Personal Aura*. Quest Books, Wheaton, Illinois, 1991.

This book contains excellent illustrations of the human aura in sickness and in health, youth and old age, including persisting thought forms.

Meek, George W., editor. *Healers and the Healing Process*. Theosophical Publishing House, Wheaton, Illinois, 1977.

Engrossing stories of healers and healing in various cultures around the world.

Powell, A. E. *The Etheric Double, The Astral Body, The Mental Body, The Causal Body and The Ego*. Theosophical Publishing House, Wheaton, Illinois, 1927.

These four books are detailed delineations of the subtle bodies, written in the language of the Theosophists. They are difficult reading but worth the effort.

Ritchie, George. *Return from Tomorrow*. Gleneida Publications, Tarrytown, New York, 1983 (paperback).

A physician's detailed description of his own near-death experience undergone when he was a youth in the army, this book contains fascinating details concerning the astral plane and is absorbing and inspirational reading.

Spink, Katryn. *I Need Souls Like You: Sharing in the Work of Mother Teresa Through Prayer and Suffering*. Harper & Row, San Francisco, 1984.

If you do not yet understand how the Law of Sacrifice works, this book will help make the concept clear to you. We are so used to thinking that being of help to others requires action, we lose sight of how valuable our thoughts are when dedicated to a high purpose.

Wilder, Thornton. *The Bridge at San Luis Rey*. Harper & Row, New York, 1955.

The library might be the best place to find this endearing fictional classic portraying the rich harvest of good that emerges from a seemingly senseless tragedy.

Acknowledgments

For this newest incarnation of *Why . . . ?* in the United States, deepest thanks to my heaven-sent agent, Brie Burkeman, and to both Joel Fotinos and his assistant at Tarcher, Andrew Yackira.

Also, to my darling daughter, Piper, whose mother refuses to own or operate a computer (or even a cell phone!)—thanks for doing your best to help me over each technological bump in the road.

About the Author

Robin Norwood was a licensed marriage and family therapist who worked in the field of addiction for fifteen years. She specialized in treating co-alcoholism and relationship addiction. She is a bestselling author with books in print throughout the world.

If you enjoyed this book from Tarcher/Penguin, then check out . . .

WOMEN WHO LOVE TOO MUCH

by Robin Norwood

Available in eBook (ISBN: 9781101222416)